beans, BISCUITS, FAMILY & friends

LIFE STORIES

BILL GOODMAN

INTERNATIONAL
RRP
PUBLISHING & DIGITAL MEDIA

RRP International Publishing LLC
Richmond/Lexington, Ky.

RRP International LLC, DBA Eugenia Ruth LLC
330 Eastern Bypass
Ste #1 Box 302
Richmond, Ky. 40475

www.rrpinternational.org

Cover design by **Jody Beamer**

Joseph Downing photos courtesy of
© **The Downing Museum/Jerry E. Baker Foundation, Inc.**

ISBN-13: 978-0-9898848-9-1

Previous Books:

God's House Calls: Finding God Through My Patients

Take More Naps (And 100 Other Life Lessons)

The Art of Opinion Writing: Insider Secrets from Top Op-Ed Columnists

The Art of Column Writing: Insider Secrets from Art Buchwald, Dave Barry, Arianna Huffington, Pete Hamill and Other Great Columnists

Don McNay's Greatest Hits: Ten Years as an Award-Winning Columnist

Life Lessons from Cancer

Son of a Son of a Gambler: Joe McNay 80ᵗʰ Birthday Edition

Life Lessons from the Golf Course: The Quest for Spiritual Meaning, Psychological Understanding and Inner Peace through the Game of Golf

Life Lessons from the Lottery: Protecting Your Money in a Scary World

Wealth Without Wall Street: A Main Street Guide to Making Money

Dedication

To my wife Debbie and my parents Henry and Eleanor Goodman

Table of Contents

Travels with Henry: Dad, Me, and Country Stores

"Grab that Baby Ruth box and run back into the store and get those 'two-for-one' Hershey deal sheets on my desk," Dad muttered as he struggled to lift a case of drinking cups into the trunk of his leaf-green, two-door, 1954 Chevrolet Bel Air Sedan. The case fit easily in the massive trunk, which was strewn with an assortment of items to be delivered to customers: a case of kitchen matches, six cans of hairspray, two dozen cans of Van Camp's Beanee Weenees, a hodgepodge of cigarette cartons, two cans of Prince Albert Smoking tobacco, and a couple of tubes of Copenhagen moist snuff. Teenage boys in Cumberland County, Kentucky, put just a pinch of that stuff between their lip and gum, and old ladies out in the country would dip too. When I was about eight years old, the first and last time I tried it, I threw up all over my cousin Charlie.

It was the summer of 1958, just past 6:30 on Tuesday morning. An overnight rain had left the asphalt parking lot of the Goodman Candy Company with just enough moisture so that a faint mist curled up around the Chevy as if it were going to jump in the car and ride down the road with us. And, since it was Tuesday, the destination was Burkesville and Eighty Eight, Summer Shade, Mud Lick, Marrowbone, and all points, on paved and unpaved roads, in between.

It was the same trip my dad had made every Tuesday for 25 years. On that particular morning, he seemed as anxious to get in the car and start as he had when he made the first trip to Cumberland County years ago. He knew that his customers, many of whom had become lifelong friends and almost family, would be eager to place orders, catch up on the news from Glasgow, and exchange a tale or two with "the candy man." He had become part of their families. He knew their children by name. He attended their funerals, and he purchased raffle tickets from the local Lions Club. He had a connection to rural folk.

At one time, the family farm was the image people had of rural life in Kentucky. Small towns dotted the landscape and connected farms throughout the state, from the hilly terrain of eastern Kentucky to the undulating countryside of the central part of the state to the fertile, rich river bottoms in the western counties. The family farm was more than plowed fields and livestock; generations born and raised on farms believed in traditional values and had a passionate attachment to the land. Kentucky poet, essayist, and author Wendell Berry has lived and farmed in Henry County for close to 40 years. He writes often of "a sense of place."

In an interview with *Mother Earth News* years ago, Berry said he'd like to get people back in touch with the realities of a farming life: "There's a great argument going on today about whether or not the family farm is going to survive or should survive. The primary concern has to be with the cultural relation between people and land." Berry added, "We need to be talking about family farmers who live on and care for small tracts of land out of the motivation that long association and deep knowledge can produce, people who know the difference between duty and love."

My father was connected to the rural life by both—love and duty. His devotion took him to the rural parts of south-central Kentucky to the farmers and proprietors of country stores. He also had a genuine love for the people and the places that had always been part of his life.

Country stores, which at one time were as common in rural Kentucky as chickens running free in the front yard, were a part of that sense of place. Today, country stores have all but disappeared, shuttered and boarded up. If you find a store at all in the countryside today, it's often dressed up with neon lights flashing "Lottery Tickets Sold Here," offering cardboard-tasting sandwiches, shrink-wrapped in shiny plastic pretending to be freshly made bologna or country ham. They wouldn't be at all like the sandwiches you could get at any number of real country stores in rural Kentucky not too long ago. My dad introduced me to these stores and sandwiches as a youngster.

I dashed back into the warehouse to pick up the samples and the Hershey sale sheet. I heard Dad exclaim, with mild aggravation,

"Dad-gum-it, we've got to get on the road." He knew we were staring at a 13-hour day. I hurried into his office through the sliding glass doors, which opened to a Taj Mahal of goods: tobacco products, household and restaurant supplies, beef jerky, and hot fudge sundae toppings (maraschino cherries, crushed peanuts, and milk chocolate syrup). My childhood friends (and later a high school girlfriend with a sweet tooth) loved visiting the warehouse with me. Their fathers had "normal" jobs as lawyers, doctors, schoolteachers. When we were younger, heading on our bikes to the library or ball field for an afternoon game, we'd stop in at the warehouse for a quick hello and a treat, which Dad always had close by.

If the workers weren't loading delivery trucks, we'd be granted floor privileges to wander the aisles. My buddies were mesmerized. Sugary candy, bubble gum, and lollipops danced in their heads, their eyes as big as saucers. We began a slow walk through temptation, aisle after aisle: 36-count bags of M&Ms, plain and peanut; PEZ, with its funny little figure-head dispenser that spit tiny pieces of tangy candy; Pixy Stixs, with a powdery sweetness that flooded the mouth—it was all there. If we were lucky, we might find a loose carton of caramel-covered Cracker Jacks popcorn with a surprise—a spinning top or paper tattoo—waiting at the bottom of every box.

The multitude of candy bars stacked in tidy rows was enough to produce gallons of chocolate, caramel, nougat, and peanuts to fill a large swimming pool several times over, from Snickers, Reese's Peanut Butter Cups and Junior Mints to Hershey's, Milky Way and the Three Musketeers. Shelves were stocked with BB Bats, Banana Splits, Black Jack Gum, Charm Pops, Chuckles, Cherryheads, Certs, Goo Goos, Goobers, Gummy Bears, and Gummy Worms.

In another section, it was as if Mr. Peanut himself was walking down the row with us. There seemed to be no end in sight to the treats that appeared: peanut brittle, peanut-butter bars, peanut-butter kisses, clusters, and patties…and then pecan pies, pralines, and pecan log rolls.

I was a popular kid and had a lot of friends. Now, I know why.

My sisters and I grew up in our father's company. Whiling away the hours, we rollerskated the smooth concrete floors until we were tired. Then we turned to games of hide-and-seek among stacks of cardboard boxes and cartons that in one minute were a secret fort and in the next transformed into a magic castle high on a mountaintop.

It was not a workplace for us. It was a mythical maze of secret doors and hidden passages where we could watch Midnight, the warehouse's resident cat, play with mice, and where on humid July afternoons we could sneak into the cooling room where chocolate bars were stored (in summer, the blazing Kentucky sun transformed the metal building into a hothouse).

Since 1933, Goodman Candy Company had existed in three principal locations in the city of Glasgow. For a time, my father had a wood-frame storefront on South Race Street, just off the town square, down the street from the Plaza Movie Theatre and next door to Lessenberry Building Supply.

When I was a toddler, Dad would roust me out of bed at dawn to ride piggy-back to a nearby car dealership where he stored his 1940s vintage station wagon, the company delivery van. He would pack and sort his supplies as he got ready for the day on the road. His second location and first real warehouse was a few streets south of that location, near the only school in town, the Baptist church, and the library. It was a concrete-block building, stretched long and narrow between Miller's Dry Cleaning and a parking lot that backed up to Shorty's DX Service Station. It had a garage-door entrance in back where the trucks could pull in for loading. Near the indoor driveway was a long wooden table—15 feet in length—where the cigarette stamping machine sat.

A small sticker that said "Candy is Delicious Food" invited guests into the showroom and office. A large roll-top oak desk dominated an area behind a narrow counter. The desk's craftsmanship was top-notch. Twelve pigeon-hole compartments contained checks and paperwork. The desk had useful filing space and even a fake drawer, which opened to reveal additional storage labeled with tiny brass plates.

In a few years, with the business growing and the product line expanding, Dad had to relocate and construct a new office and warehouse south of town. He became one of the first businessmen to build on the highway bypass, in an expansive light-blue corrugated aluminum structure with a much larger area for product display, offices, and storage. Despite a bigger store, my dad, who had nurtured the company's growth through the Depression, World War II, and into the 1950s, kept things the same.

I grabbed the samples Dad had sent me to retrieve and met him back in the parking lot.

"Come on, son, we're a day late and a dollar short," he said. "We've got to get a move on."

Dad had on his uniform: dress pants, not jeans (I never saw him wear blue jeans), a short-sleeved shirt, a tie (he wore a tie seven days a week), a plastic pocket protector for pens and pencils, and his ever-present felt fedora, purchased from Jolly's Men's Store on the square uptown. His brown working shoes were slightly worn, but always polished.

If Dad was particular about his dress, he wasn't about his car. His automobiles were rolling offices, stocked with order blanks, extra pens, and samples. They also served as delivery vehicles when a customer needed something before the scheduled arrival of the warehouse truck. His autos were just, well, transportation— something that would get him from one store to the next, across a shallow creek or up the steep grade to the Alpine Motel in Burkesville. His cars were nondescript, dull in color, and equipped with the bare essentials: manually operated windows, a spare tire, and an antenna—and a radio. He loved cruising along the highway after a hard day's work listening to a Cincinnati Reds or St. Louis Cardinals baseball game. When announcers Jack Buck or Dizzy Dean were riding shotgun with him, it was even better.

He drove his cars until the wheels fell off. In one of them, an old dark green Chevrolet with tattered cloth seats and a back-seat window that wouldn't roll up all the way, the heel of his shoe wore a hole the size of a silver dollar through the floor board just behind the accelerator. You could see the pavement through the hole and, when it rained, water splashed up through the opening, dampening Daddy's cuff. He didn't mind at all.

I climbed up into the dusty Bel Air, pushed a few boxes and papers out of the way, and settled in for the road trip out Highway 90, southeast toward Burkesville and the Tennessee line.

"Don't let me forget to get that case of cups out of the trunk this afternoon when we get to the Dairy Freeze. He thinks the entire student population at Cumberland County High School will stop by for a milkshake this afternoon, and he'll run out of cups before our truck gets here tomorrow," Dad said.

"Yes sir," I responded as I made an entry in the tiny notebook that fit in the back pocket of my jeans. (The son of the owner could get away with casual attire.)

Our first stop that morning was in Eighty Eight, a strangely named town in Kentucky. According to the *New York Times*, it was named in 1860 by the community's first postmaster, Dabnie Nunnally. He had little faith in the legibility of his handwriting and thought that using numbers would solve the problem. He reached into his pants pocket and came up with 88 cents.

One of Dad's oldest and most loyal customers was Mr. Robert Richardson, who had been a customer since Dad started his wholesale business. I grabbed a carton of hairspray out of the trunk, and Dad hoisted his boxes of samples out of the back seat, balancing them under his left arm as he reached for his order pad with the other hand. Mr. Richardson greeted us with a grin.

"I see you brought along some good help," he said, giving me a pat on the shoulder. "Good help is hard to find these days."

"I need someone to help with the driving," Dad responded.

Richardson's store was similar to hundreds of country stores that were once part of the rural landscape. Most people went to town, Glasgow or Burkesville, periodically to buy supplies or find items that the country stores didn't carry. But my dad remembers stories about how most of the inventory, like crackers, used to come in barrels and metal containers. At one time, coffee was shipped green, and homemakers roasted it before it was ready to brew. Meats were packed in salt and had to be cured. Many essentials, like milk and butter, weren't available because there was no refrigeration. A gallon of kerosene cost a nickel. Cornmeal, flour, sugar, salt, baking soda, baking powder, and hard candy would send a farmer to the store. But when you lived and worked in the country, you raised just about everything else for the family table. A few years later that began to change. Grocery store wholesalers offered boxed macaroni, canned salmon, and pizza supplies. Little Italy arrived in Mud Lick.

If there was no general store in an area, life could be difficult for farmers. Country stores provided small communities with goods and services such as newspapers from the city and a post office. The stores helped a community by attracting other businesses—auto and tractor repair, churches, and restaurants. General stores not only attracted people to the community, they became the center of social life. Farming was solitary work, and the store gave people a chance to visit, catch up on the local gossip, and discuss weather and crops. Country-store porches often had a bench or rocking chairs where customers could chat and pass the time.

When I traveled with Dad, he talked about what he remembered from growing up in the country. He spent summers on the farm, and in winter he and his mother stayed with relatives so he could attend school.

On that morning, as we motored down the main highway, the road ahead seemed to disappear in the early-morning haze. Dad looked at me, the smoke curling from a newly lit Lucky Strike, fedora pulled low on his brow, and gave me a history lesson in Country Store 101.

"Early country stores were simple, two-story wood-frame buildings; some never got painted. But they wanted to be noticed, so to make them look taller, some store owners attached a façade, or false front, to the top of the store," he said.

I savored learning this new word—façade—from him.

"And you know what? That's why we say 'puttin' up a good front' when someone thinks you're acting a little different than usual. Somebody told me that a long time ago."

I marveled over the things my dad knew.

During the years I traveled with Dad, the exteriors and interiors of the country stores we serviced changed. But on occasion, when you left the main highway and drove two or three miles on a secondary road, you might find, say in Holland or Mount Herman, a store that advertised "groceries, hardware, dry goods, clothing and shoes" on its false front. And you'd truly find those things inside.

At Sturdivant's, a copper-colored brass bell tinkled our arrival as we strolled through the front door. While Dad showed Mr. Sturdivant samples, I wandered through the aisles, taking in everything, from rows of canned goods, spices, cake mix, and bread to the clothing department in the back. Shoes, brogans—a heavy, sturdy, ankle-high work boot I would later wear when cutting tobacco—and a selection of ladies' footwear occupied one section; work shirts, overalls, and socks filled another; hats and caps hung on wooden knobs along the wall. Long wooden counters stretched along both sides of the store. On one side, a section had been divided for kitchen goods, pots, pans and dishes. Another was like a miniature Walgreen's, stocked high with Bayer aspirin, cough drops, and Carter's Little Liver Pills. At the back of the store, a modern, glass-enclosed refrigerator unit contained jumbo blocks of cheese—American, Swiss, Pepper Jack—and meats—bologna, liverwurst, turkey breasts, and roast beef. Whopping glass jars of pickled eggs and dill pickles sat on top of the unit. A side door opened into a small room that housed hardware, bolts, screws, hammers and nails, garden seed, bulk cattle feed, and deworming medicine for cattle.

Near the front of the store, on the top of the other wooden counter sat a mammoth cast-iron cash register. It stood about two-and-a-half feet tall with a large handle on the right side that turned the numbers, dollars, and cents signs in the glass window on the top. When the handle was brought down, the main compartment with the cash drawer would pop open with a clatter. Beside the register were rows of glass jars filled with suckers—Tootsie Pops, Charms Blow Pops— Jolly Ranchers, Atomic Fireballs, Sweet Tarts.

"Okay, Henry, let's get to it," Mr. Sturdivant would say. "If you're going to get an order from me today, now's the time 'cuz I got 15 baloney-and-cheese sandwiches to make for the pipeline crew, and they'll be here in about an hour."

He and Dad would walk a couple of aisles, Mr. Sturdivant calling out items he needed while Dad quickly scribbled in his order book. Some store owners would write orders and leave them for Dad to copy to his pad. Others, like Mr. Sturdivant, liked to call out the product as they shuffled through their stores. Dad might reach into a box or two and count the number that remained, asking, "What about another?" He almost always got a nod. He knew the product line well, what sold, and what might gather dust. So when Dad suggested they stock up, they did.

On that day, I wandered to the rear of the store where Mrs. Sturdivant was putting up the mail.

"Billy, you're gettin' to be as tall as your daddy," she said, making only a slight exaggeration. "Come here, and help me put up these letters."

Outside of medium-size towns during the 1950s, Kentucky post offices were still located in the general store. Each family had a cubbyhole for receiving letters and packages. When mail arrived, the storekeeper sorted it and put it up. Before there were rural paper routes, morning and afternoon newspapers were delivered by mail and not always on the same day, though the paper eventually got there.

Mrs. Sturdivant knew if she didn't get the mail put up as soon as it arrived, she'd have locals hanging around, looking over her shoulder, asking for it. She also knew that if they received a newspaper or Sears and Roebuck catalogue, they might just sit down, order a sandwich, an RC cola and a moon pie, and while away a few hours before they got back to farming.

Although Dad was courteous to every customer, he learned early on that time was money. Regardless of the kinship he might have with a store owner, he needed to get on his way. There were many stops to make before nightfall.

He developed an entrepreneurial spirit early in life when his father's death in the 1918 influenza outbreak required him to work to help support his mother. As a teenager, he learned from an uncle and cousins at Goodman Brothers, a wholesale business located just off the square in Glasgow. Uncle Will became a mentor to Dad, part teacher, part substitute father, and part Groucho Marx. A jokester, Uncle Will seemed to have an apt phrase or funny description for every occasion.

During the Depression, Uncle Will and cousins Charlie and Joe fell on hard times and closed Goodman Brothers. Will went out on his own and was a well-known salesman in Southern Kentucky, staying on the road until he was almost 80. When he got too old to drive, he hired his grandsons to motor him all the way to London, where they would overnight, or to one of his lifelong customers in LaFollette, Tennessee. Uncle Will was a broker for several national brands: Fleetwood Coffee out of Nashville, the Hampton Cracker Company in Iowa, and Sue Bee Honey.

Uncle Will might have been called a peddler or a huckster,

both of which had a kinder connotation then they do today. Most likely, he ran into other itinerant salesmen selling all kinds of patent medicine: salve, liniment, headache pills, laxatives, and compounds to sugar-cure meat. Huckster vans visited rural Kentucky until the 1950s. Dad said the vans were shaped like school buses without the side windows. Inside a bus was an aisle with counters on each side and shelves above with leather straps stretched across the front to keep the goods from falling.

Hucksters planned their routes so they would make weekly stops, although some areas were served by more than one peddler. Sometimes, the vans stopped at county schools. Kids would pool their money and buy snacks or a cookie that they couldn't get at home. The trucks were crammed with a surprisingly complete line of goods. At Christmas, a huckster might bring fresh fruit to a farm family or offer piece goods and needle and thread to the lady of the house.

During World War II, hucksters carried the same items that country stores offered. Dad, whose bad eyesight kept him out of the war, said various items were rationed during the war. Hershey cut back on its chocolate, and some brands of cigarettes were hard to come by.

"I believe we're going to hit Burkesville on Sidewalk Days," Dad said as we motored across the county lines of Barren, Metcalfe, Adair. "The traffic might slow us down."

On Sidewalk Days, Burkesville merchants hauled clothing, furniture, and whatever they couldn't sell inside their store out to the sidewalk to sell at reduced prices. In many counties, a kind of farmers' market came to be associated with the one day of the month that the county court was in session. Farmers would come to town to take care of business and to socialize. Cattle were brought to the stockyard on those days, too. Dad told me about one little town that doubled its small population on Mule Day, a special celebration when you could buy, sell, or swap a mule. Court days were also known for trading pocketknives, firearms, and dogs, although on this blistering July morning, I only saw farmers searching for a shady spot where they could kill some time before returning to work.

The town square in Burkesville was similar to others in rural Kentucky at the time. Dad had cultivated his business with care over the years. At gasoline service stations, he unlocked the candy and cigarette machines, and filled them with product. Candy and gum that didn't fit in the machine were stored in a small compartment just below the knobs and coin slots.

He wrote up the order, noting that Planter's Salted Peanuts and "Nabs," the round crackers filled with peanut butter, had sold out. He ordered a dozen Gordon's Potato Chips that would arrive on the truck the next day.

At the corner drugstore, which still had a full-service counter and soda fountain, Dad made a notation in his order pad for drinking straws, napkins, plastic spoons, and marshmallow topping, a sweet, spongy signature on the ice-cream indulgences of adults and children alike.

Growing up, I wasn't allowed to frequent the Glasgow pool hall. But on trips with Dad, the rules changed. As a youngster, my dad had learned to shoot pool in a pool hall in Glasgow, but he decided to teach me the rudiments of the game on a miniature table I got for Christmas one year. There were two or three billiard parlors on the square in Burkesville. They were grimy, smoky rooms with as many as six pool tables jammed together in a narrow building with grease from fried bologna sandwiches and French fries coating the walls and ceiling—but they were customers.

Dad would holler at Pete, the fry cook and manager, raising his voice over the din of clanking pool balls being racked for another game. "Looks like you need some cigars."

Pete, a wad of chewing tobacco crowding his jaw and making him hard to understand, answered. "Gimme a couple boxes of King Edward, a Dutch Master, uh, Tampa Nugget and a Tiparillo, a card of them pipes, Dr. something or other (Dr. Grabow), some Kentucky Club pipe tobacco, two Copenhagen, two Skoal, and a box of Warren County and Mammoth Cave, small and large twist." As he finished up, he looked around for a place to discard the increasingly raunchy pool of tobacco juice that was spilling over a section of his lower lip.

"How about your restaurant supplies?" Dad shouted.

"Nah, we ain't sellin' nothin' up here."

Was it possible folks had the same thoughts that had crossed my mind about eating lunch here?

"Gimme a case of crackers and some cigarettes, that's all I need today," Phil said. "Doubt I can pay for that."

Dad gave me a little grin.

There was a real difference being in a small town for a few hours compared to being on the road from store to store. In Burkesville, a sleepy little town nestled in the Cumberland River Valley with a population of around 2000, there were things to see, drugstore soda fountains to visit, comic books to read, and friendships to be renewed.

There was also the Alpine Motel, which advertised "Breathtaking Views from Every Suite." While Dad took the order, I had time to look at old photographs on the lobby wall and learn the story of the "first great American oil well" found in the shallows of the Cumberland River in the early part of the 1800s. Historians confirm that the well was being drilled for salt deposits and just happened to hit "black gold." That kind of fact is what a small town uses for marketing when little else has happened there.

I looked forward to eating with Dad because he always chose just the right spot, with the tastiest food and most satisfying drink for the free time we had before getting back on the highway.

When we walked into the Do-Drop-In Café on the square in Burkesville, the aroma at the door was of meat loaf, fluffy mashed potatoes, and heavenly pinto beans, flavored with a slice or two of hog jowl or bacon. Waitresses served the meal home-style on long tables where neighbors and strangers alike could break bread together. No sooner had we sat down than a gregarious waitress with a wide grin and a beehive hairdo would bring us fresh, hot biscuits. A piece of lemon meringue pie sat on the counter, safely ensconced under a glass dome. It was all there for the taking for $1.25. What a deal.

Some days we found ourselves off the main highway on a gravel road around noon with no decent lunch spot for miles. In small, one-man repair garages or bait shops, I watched men open cans of Van Camp's Beanee Weenees and spoon hot dogs and pork 'n beans with one hand while fiddling with a cracked engine block with the other. Beans, a Butternut bar, and a Pepsi were lunch.

In every town with a population over 300, there were the ice-cream emporiums with names like Dairy-O, Tasty Freeze, or Dairy Queen. Burger Broil and Tommy's T-Burger served tater-tots, a Mexican hamburger, and a vanilla shake through a tiny, screened window. On Friday nights after high school football and Saturday nights after the movie, these were the cruising spots in town. You never knew when you might get lucky and get a wink from the captain of the cheerleading squad.

Dad enjoyed a bowl of pinto beans and cornbread at a sit-down restaurant, but it was the country-store food that was his favorite. After talking with the owner, showing his samples, and writing down the order for tomorrow's delivery, Dad would ask: "You ready for a little lunch?" And I would always nod.

Country stores had an endless variety of inexpensive cuisine. Posted on the wall behind the counter was a menu board with the price of a slice of cheese or bologna on white bread—and back then, it was always white bread—a fresh turkey sandwich, and a bag of chips. Some people would drive for miles just to have a slice of liverwurst for dinner. But Dad was a simple man and more times than not, he would have cheese and crackers. The cracker was square, with a thin slice of American cheese on top and another square cracker on top of the cheese. That was it—it didn't even have mayonnaise. Some days, when he wanted a change, he ordered a slice of Swiss cheese. An RC Cola and a moon pie would round out his early-afternoon repast. With his cracker sandwich wrapped in waxed paper, he went out on the front porch if the weather permitted, where he billed a few orders, talked to locals about their tobacco crop, and enjoyed the day.

He was a happy man.

When I was 12, a day as a junior traveling salesman had a way of wearing me out, but Dad never faltered or let on he was the least bit tired. We finished our rounds in Burkesville, made a few stops on the outskirts of town, and then turned that big Chevrolet around and headed for home. The route to Glasgow took us a different way, on another rural highway where we made additional stops. After a carton of chocolate milk and a candy bar to tide me over until suppertime, I got sleepy, bouncing around on a curvy road with an early-evening summer breeze streaming in the window.

Around four or five o'clock, after another stop or two—Dad said, "Why don't you stay in the car, read your book. This won't take long."

I yawned, stretched out, and shut my eyes for a few minutes.

Heading home, the highway took us over small streams and bridges, winding its way by the edge of cornfields and dairy cows slowly making their way to the milking barn. Often, a farm tractor headed toward us. We regularly had to slow down so the farmer could swing the tractor wide to turn into the lane taking him home.

Dad's muscular left arm, resting on the open window of the car door, was tan up to the point where his sleeve touched the skin. I observed his "farmer's wave" from my vantage point across the front seat. He never passed another vehicle without raising the first two fingers of his left hand and, ever so slightly, lifting the first and second digits a couple of inches, dipping them for an instant, and then bringing them back down again.

"Who was that?" I'd inquire.

"Oh, I don't know. Just being friendly, I guess. Never hurts to be friendly," he'd reply.

I'm sorry to say that there was a time in my teenage years when I was embarrassed that Dad would wave at complete strangers.

There was a particular section of Highway 90 that seemed to characterize all that was simple and good about those trips. Although the road curved around hills and snaked back and forth between country stores, one section just before Marrowbone opened up to a broad, expansive, and verdant valley sustained for decades by the crystal-clear Beaver Creek. Driving southwest from Glasgow, you'd top a hill and be ushered slowly down the slope for a couple of miles before bottoming out in the village. No flashing caution lights, no sirens. Just schoolchildren, farmers, bankers, and ordinary folks going about their business.

"Have you given much thought about coming into the business when you get a little older? It's not a bad life. You're not going to get rich, but you'll have enough to put food on the table," Dad would ask me with a laugh. "And you get Sundays off. I'm thinking about closing up on Saturdays at two. I got a call last night from Dusty Miller asking if I'd coach your Little League baseball team—what would you think about that?" He continued, "You know, this is hard work, but I like the people, and I can tell they like you. You'll be driving before too long. Someday you'll make this trip on your own."

It would be a long time before I would make the trip on my own. The journey belonged to my father back then. But he was willing to share it with me.

Living on Cornbread and Pinto Beans

"If God had meant cornbread to be sweet, he'd have called it cake."
-Mark Twain

My dad loved his family, the Baptist church, and his work. But ranking right up there close to the top was cornbread.

Whatever cornbread you grew up on is probably the one you consider perfect. When someone mentions cornbread, if you're like most people, you probably find yourself exclaiming, "Cornbread? I love cornbread!"

That was what my dad always said.

Mom made him corn muffins, corn sticks baked in a cast-iron cornstick pan, cornmeal corncakes fried on a griddle, skillet cornbread or pone, a thick, malleable cornmeal dough, a pancake-like bread baked in the oven, and hot water dodgers (little oval cornmeal cakes). I believe he could have lived his entire life on a bowl of pinto beans and cornbread.

With a grin on his face as bright as a ray of sunshine, he would reach for a wedge of skillet cornbread and delicately, intently, break his treasure into small bites and crumbs, which he sprinkled on top of the beans. When Mom fixed a mess of greens, like kale or boiled cabbage for dinner, Dad thought there was nothing better in the world than a stack of corncakes in the center of the table waiting for a dab of butter to be spread carefully over the circumference of the cake. If my sister and I had taken a bite or two of cabbage and finished our glasses of milk, we were rewarded with the privilege of pouring maple syrup on our cake. Today, cornbread is one of those foods that has stood the test of time. Like a Southern writer's fictional heroes, it has endured.

In 1950, in the first new house she had ever lived in, my mother took on the responsibility of being chief architect and kitchen designer. I'm sure she wanted a kitchen for more than just making cornbread, but that could have been part of her thinking. She knew exactly what to tell the builders. It was well before granite countertops and fancy fixtures. At that time, the kitchen wasn't meant to be part of a family room or a central gathering place; its job was to be functional. It was a plain room with a simple stove and refrigerator she used to prepare meals for her busy family.

My mother's kitchen, in our stone, ranch-style home, was tiny by today's standards, but it was all she needed to mix up a little seasoning, celery, and fresh ground beef for her signature meat loaf, which she topped off with a dab of homemade tomato sauce. The pantry was stocked with all the sweet ingredients—brown sugar, chocolate chips, and vanilla—for blonde brownies that had a way of calling our name when we got within a mile of the house. The room was Mom's creation. She had chosen a light azure to calm her through the hours she labored in her cook's room: it was the color of her cabinets, wallpaper, and window trim. A small hutch sat against a back wall chock-full of pans, ladles, and long-handled spoons she used when performing her magic.

Today, when I think of home I think of Mom in her kitchen, apron tied neatly in the back with an ever-present handkerchief tucked in a front pocket, puttering around her petite cooking quarters. This I know to be true—my mother's devotion to traditional food and drink of the South and the rituals surrounding their consumption are my most defining and enduring recollections of being brought up in rural Kentucky. Although I live in a city now, small-town life still lives in me.

Meanwhile, there's a lot to know about cornbread.

Food historians tell us that when Captain John Smith stepped on the Virginia shore in the early 1600s, he was introduced to two of the oldest, most basic, and most vital food sources ever known in human history: pigs and corn. The meeting of the English and the Indians at Jamestown and the subsequent intermingling of their foods marked the beginning of American cookery, and more specifically, the regional food of the South.

Corn had been cultivated in the New World for so long that the Indians had no memory of its origin. The immigrant population soon learned the value of corn and how to use it to make ashcake, hoecakes, corn dodgers, cornpone, hominy, grits and, of course, cornbread.

Fifty years ago, a food writer for *Progressive Farmer's Southern Cookbook* wrote, "To try to cook without cornmeal in the South is a lost cause. Aside from cornbread which many Southerners make once a day, we need 'meal' to fry fish or squirrel. We use meal in chess pie and most 'dressings' or stuffings. We use cornmeal dumplings for turnip greens and poke salad. Many will tell you that fried chicken must be dipped in cornmeal."

So, cornbread has a long, deep history in the South and in the Appalachian mountains. The reasons are not at all clear. Some say the explanation is simply that cooks in the South, like my mother, consistently made superior cornbread. Yankee cornbread, made from yellow cornmeal, just doesn't measure up. Southerners tend to favor white meal and use sugar and flour sparingly, if at all.

Southern food can be perplexing to those who live north of the Mason-Dixon line, even more so to those from beyond the United States. My older sister, Charlotte, attended college at Lake Erie in Painesville, Ohio. During a semester break, she brought her Asian American roommate to visit Kentucky. Mom prepared a delicious supper: fresh green beans, creamy mashed potatoes, fixed pork chops—drizzled with milk gravy—and cornbread muffins. This beautiful young woman sat down at the table with us and stared rather uncomfortably at her plate.

"Well, I hope everything looks and tastes good. It's so nice to have you with us, Lida," Mom said in her most welcoming and charming manner.

"Yes, thank you."

I could see my sister had noticed Lida's uneasiness.

"Hope you like pork chops," Charlotte said, cutting into the first one she'd had in months. Mom had fried them with a little flour and cornmeal dusting. They smelled divine.

Lida looked up sheepishly from her plate. "I've never had a pork chop."

Blank stares and silence. *She'd never eaten a pork chop.*

"And this will be my first taste of cornbread, too. Charlotte told me what a great cook you were and that your cornbread muffins would melt in my mouth."

And she's never had cornbread.

My younger sister and I giggled just a bit. It turned out that Lida loved both the pork and the cornbread.

Cornbread complemented our dinner that evening just as it had nourished many through the Great Depression. It had been a staple on the tables of coal miners during booms and busts, and had been prized in Kentucky homes like mine for decades.

When was the last time you went in a restaurant and found any variation of cornbread on the menu? And even if you dropped into a roadside café or a Southern eatery in a place like New Orleans, for example, you might find cornbread, but I'll bet you wouldn't find hot water dodgers. They're a relic of the past. Abraham Lincoln was raised on these little oval cornmeal cakes. George Washington Carver took them to school, and Rooster Cogburn used them for target practice in Charles Portis's book *True Grit:*

"Rooster set about preparing our supper. Here is what he brought along for 'grub': a sack of salt and a sack of red pepper and a sack of taffy—all this in his jacket pockets—and then some ground coffee beans and a big slab of salt pork and one hundred and seventy corn dodgers. I could scarcely credit it. The 'corn dodgers' were balls of what might be called hot-water cornbread. Rooster said the woman who prepared them thought the order was for a wagon party of marshals. 'Well,' he said, 'when they get too hard to eat plain we can make mush from them and what we have left we can give to the stock.' He made some coffee in a can and fried some pork. Then he sliced up some of the dodgers and fried the pieces in grease. Fried bread! That was a new dish to me. He and LeBoeuf made fast work of about a pound of pork and a dozen dodgers."

Portis was a Southerner and must have had hot water dodgers when he was growing up in Arkansas. *True Grit*, his second novel, was serialized by *The Saturday Evening Post* in 1968. Along with *Look* and *Life* magazines, *The Saturday Evening Post* was in my home and read by my mother religiously. But she was frying hot water cornbread in her kitchen well before that time.

Just like Rooster Cogburn's chuck-wagon cook, Mom regularly faced a hot skillet: hers sat on her four-burner, two-door oven stove. She would ready about six handfuls of white cornmeal, a half-teaspoon of salt, and about a tablespoon of lard or bacon grease—left over from breakfast—mix it well, and set it aside. Boiling hot water was added to stiffen the mixture, maybe a little milk or cream. Then, as carefully as a sculptor might form a neoclassical masterpiece, she would divide the mix into portions and "dodge" the round mounds of cornmeal from hand to hand until she plopped them onto the sizzling skillet. Only seconds passed before she would turn the dodgers with a spatula, lifting them from the stove and piling them on a serving platter. They were miniature Michelangeloes—works of art molded by my mother in her own studio.

Corn Dodgers

6 handfuls of white cornmeal

½ teaspoon salt

1 tablespoon lard

bacon drippings

Combine ingredients. Pour in enough boiling water to make a stiff mixture. Mix well and cool. Divide into six portions and "dodge" from hand to hand to shape. Have a well-greased griddle hot. Place dodgers on griddle, and fry until crispy on both sides.

Simple. Quick. Thin. Not fancy, not complicated. But biting into the crunchy crust of a hot water dodger was a little bit of heaven transposed in a small kitchen in South Central Kentucky, in a time and place that no longer remains, but will always be remembered.

Growing Killer Tomatoes

I've never been a farmer. I'm not a master gardener. Sometimes, I get kumquats and cucumbers mixed up. But I do know tomatoes, peaches, cantaloupe, sweet summer onions, summer squash, cabbage, broccoli, and Kentucky runner green beans fresh from the farm.

At least I know their taste and smell.

Just because you grow up in rural America doesn't necessarily mean you know agriculture or anything about beans and "taters."

Growing up in the rural South, I took it for granted that fresh vegetables, farm eggs, and country ham were grown and cured just a few miles from our house. When I lived in the country, no one went out of their way to point that out or talk about freshness, organically grown produce, or free-range chickens. If someone had mentioned free-range chickens to me when I was nine, I might have flashed on Tom Mix or Tonto riding through western Montana chasing a giant fowl with a lasso. It just wasn't relevant.

It is, however, the tomato that takes its place at the head of the table. The tomato is the one, true warm-weather fruit (yes, a fruit) that we rush to plant in spring. Then we brag about its size and savor its freshness and taste throughout summer. The tomato is a gift from the gods. It is planted with reverence and hope that the green, scrawny stem will take root, flourish, and bear globes of goodness in the hot months, producing for us slices, relish, gazpacho, and tomato pie all the way until fall.

I once came across a poem online by a woman named Bettie O'Neil. She paid tribute to the tomato when she wrote:

> Tomato so juicy
> so firm and so round
> I can hardly believe
> you came from the ground.

Filled with vitamins
light and love
my palate delights again
in my mouth you I shove

A quick Wikipedia search for the history of the tomato reveals a fascinating story. First cultivated by the native Indians of South America in prehistoric times, it moved to Mexico more than 3000 years ago when settlers migrated there. It found its way to Europe in the 16th century and grew in Italy in 1550. For a long time in America, the tomato was thought to be poisonous, a member of the nightshade family. Just think—this delectable delight, this tantalizing taste, poisonous? Preposterous.

So, it is with deep respect to "pomo d'oro," the golden apple, so named by a Sienese botanist, that I tell you of my quest to grow the killer tomato. From backyard to barnyard to downtown farmer's market, it has been and will continue to be a quest for the tomato with perfect taste, precise size, and ideal color.

I remember trying my luck with some tomato plants when I was still in high school. I have a faint recollection of stubbornly stumbling out to the backyard on a blustery, cold day in March to try and hack my way through what surely was a permafrost layer of dirt and rock. I'd read that in order to have a successful garden in the summer you had to turn the ground early in spring. I don't think I broke through the grass cover. And I don't think I ever got the plants in the ground. There would be no garden in my backyard for many years to come.

By that time, my sister Charlotte, seven years older than me, had graduated from college, come back home to teach school, and married a farmer. In many ways, I idolized her husband, Freddie. I'd never known a farmer and had only visited a farm a time or two in my life. I'd never driven a tractor, and Freddie taught me how. That worked out fine until the afternoon I drove the tractor too close to the barn gate. I hollered at Freddie to come help me get out of that fix without tearing down a wood-plank fence.

As part of my maturation on the farm, he gave me riding lessons on one of the fastest horses he owned, an Appaloosa named Devil Heart, and thought he'd done a good job teaching me how to saddle and bridle him. That was until the day Freddie, sitting tall in the saddle on his steed, suggested we race to the creek 200 yards ahead. Just after digging my heels into the side of Devil Heart, I felt the saddle begin to slide sideways until I was unceremoniously dumped onto the hard ground, a fall from grace that left me with a broken wrist. I had forgotten to tighten the cinch around the horse's belly to hold the saddle securely in place.

Freddie's mother had a big garden near her farmhouse, a rambling, two-story home with high ceilings and an expansive kitchen. When I worked in Freddie's tobacco patch, I'd always end up in "Muh's" spacious dining room table surrounded by the resident tenant and several other farm workers who had been hired to help out. At dinner during planting season in early summer, her table was heaped high with roast beef that Freddie had raised and slaughtered; dishes of onions, collards and kale; potatoes that had been stored through the winter; and green beans canned the previous summer. Tall glasses of sweet tea were poured. We might top off the meal with a slice of lemon meringue pie, eating it as we rested under the huge oak tree in the front yard. Then we'd head back to the tobacco patch to finish up planting the tiny green sprouts that grew over the summer into seven-foot tobacco plants.

Later in the summer, those same plants would be sliced off at ground level with a razor-sharp tobacco knife and impaled on a tobacco stick before being hauled on a tractor to the tobacco barn to cure before being transported to the tobacco sales in town. It was back-breaking hard work.

The only pleasurable memory I have of that end-of-summer experience was that it always landed us back in the dining room of the farmhouse for a late-summer meal of Silver Queen corn, ripe tomatoes, broccoli and fresh green beans and more sweet tea.

But it was the tomatoes I remember the most. Sliced thin, with a little salt and pepper, they had a way of making the meal complete. In some ways, it made the hot August sun and the heavy sticks of tobacco worth the trouble.

Years later when I lived in Texas with my wife and kids, our family visited a produce market we passed on the way home from church. The owners had a trick way of getting you to buy from them before state and local health departments stepped in with their rules and regulations—slicing open any piece of fruit or produce you happened to have your eye on and giving you a free sample. It made no difference if you made a purchase, they were there to please your taste buds. They knew if they cut into a fresh Dixie Red peach whose juice rolled off your tongue and down the front of your best Sunday shirt, they had made a sale. With a sharp paring knife in hand, the proprietor aimed the blade and dissected an Early Girl tomato with enough skill so as not to lose any of the delicious seeds or juice. I'd walk away with a sack of tomatoes and a ready-to-eat cantaloupe, which our family enjoyed until the next Sunday when we went right back for more.

So, why not be satisfied with the tomatoes I'd found at the produce market? Why did I feel this pull to plant my own? It could have been a "guy thing." New house, nice sunny spot in the backyard. Why not put a few plants out before the summer drought and humidity smothered most living things?

We lived outside of downtown Houston in a neighborhood off the Katy Freeway when I set out on a pursuit to grow the perfect Texas tomato. I couldn't have asked for better growing conditions: a long, hot season, good soil, plenty of sunshine. My garden hose was close to my backyard plot of land. Plants and seeds were available at the hardware store.

In early spring, I turned the ground, sprinkled in a little peat moss and carefully, almost one by one, put the seeds into the soil. I knew these seeds would turn out to produce a bountiful harvest of plump, moist fruit, making my mouth pucker with that real tomato taste I remembered from my Kentucky boyhood. I'd show these Texans a thing or two about growing a garden.

That was before I met Patty, the Ringling Bros. and Barnum & Bailey elephant. The Greatest Show on Earth was in the city for its annual tour. I'd read how elephant manure could be a great fertilizer on a vegetable garden, and the circus offered the public an opportunity to come out to the arena where they were performing nightly and pick up a few bags. What they hadn't advertised is that you had to shovel it yourself into garbage bags, haul it to your car, and drive home with the smelly stuff in the trunk. On this particular day, the temperature was approaching 95 degrees, normal for Houston in spring.

Houston was a big city with big-city smells. Located about 45 minutes from the ship channel and the Gulf of Mexico, it wasn't unusual to catch the faint odor of gas and oil barges burning off excess product or tons of solid waste being unloaded in a landfill nearby. There were manufacturing plants everywhere producing tires, auto parts, and food products. But there weren't that many locations where one could catch the fresh essence of a pachyderm's waste product other than the trunk of my vehicle.

I arrived home in the early evening, immediately unloaded the dung, and quietly spread it on the garden. For some reason, maybe because I had transported the stuff for the 30-minute round trip from circus to house, the smell seemed to have dissipated and putting it on my garden plot wasn't that unpleasant.

Until later that evening.

I had not done well in advanced chemistry in college. Formulas and scientific equations had escaped me. But, that night, I deduced that the cooler temperatures of the Texas nightfall and the hearty watering I'd given the garden before bedtime had somehow chemically reacted in a way that caused my children to cry and my neighbors to complain.

Early the next morning, using shovel, garbage bags, and clothes I would later throw away (because not even the Houston homeless wanted to wear those jeans and T-shirts after what they had been through), I began the task of scooping up and shoveling Patty's patties. I not only dug up the dung, but I gouged deeply into my preciously cultivated topsoil and discarded with abandon all of those tiny, carefully placed seeds that were just beginning to poke their little green heads up through the silt. Seeds, topsoil, plants, a few spring onions, leaf lettuce, and a few marigolds were thrown into bags and hauled to the dump. That year, there were no Texas tomatoes to write home about.

I didn't give up.

When I moved back to Kentucky, I thought maybe the soil, climate, and a little homegrown luck might produce some delicious tomatoes. Our Kentucky backyard was much larger than the small space I'd had in Houston. It was also thick with red maple, magnolia, and sycamore trees. The only sunny spot was about 50 yards from our only water supply. After carrying buckets of water back and forth from the house to the garden, I ended up stringing several lengths of hose together for a better irrigation system. The tomato plants were looking fabulous: plenty of sunshine, water, and Sevin, a chemical insect powder, to keep the bugs off.

That was until we left for vacation. The water hose had been left in the yard attached to the spigot. I had asked my niece to come over two or three times during the week we were traveling and water. Simple request, wrong outcome. Allison walked over the first Monday we were out of town, turned on the water, and didn't remember to come back for three days. The tomato plants were flooded, and so was my neighbor's patio. No tomatoes that summer.

Nanny and Papa, my wife's mother and father, were probably the best gardeners I have ever known. When Papa retired at a young age because of health reasons, they moved back to Henry County, Kentucky, near Sulphur, where they built a house and planted a big garden each spring. From early spring to late fall, visiting them was like going to see a county agent or studying agriculture from a professor. Papa knew when to plant, what to plant, and how to keep the bugs off the squash.

In the spring, after reading the Farmer's Almanac to be sure he was going to set the garden by the right phase of the moon, he planted mustard greens and kale; radishes, spring onions, early peas, and a variety of leafy lettuces; blackberries, strawberries and rhubarb; cucumbers, green peppers, hot and mild peppers; squash and several different varieties of tomatoes—Early Girls and Big Boys and at least one type guaranteed to produce by the Fourth of July.

I quizzed him on the growing methods he had perfected with his tomatoes. In the spring, the plants were laid out in long rows, some about two feet apart. As they began to take root, he would cage some of the plants while the others were free to spread and snake along the ground. He staked them using Nanny's worn pantyhose cut in long strips and tied delicately from stem to tobacco stick. Others curled in and out of metal cages that held the fruit until time for picking. The tomatoes that grew unencumbered by stake or cage were a variety used for tomato juice and Nanny's delicious relish. Papa was a PhD when it came to growing tomatoes.

While those plants were still producing, he had already tilled half of the garden, chopped up the dirt clogs from the early summer rain, and had begun to mulch and prepare the garden for summer—sweet corn, zucchini, and a tomato resistant to summer heat; cabbage, cauliflower, big yellow onions and new potatoes.

In fall, more tomatoes bore fruit past the first frost; squash and pumpkins arrived both before and after Halloween. It was an education to watch him work, to help with the weeding periodically, and to pull my chair up to the dining room table and dig in to some of Nanny's country cooking. In a flash, she could cook a roast, slice tomatoes, whip up creamy mashed potatoes, make coleslaw from scratch, mix up a batch of cornbread, string fresh green beans, and bake a blackberry cobbler. It seemed every meal was Sunday dinner.

She was an amazing cook. I don't think I've ever had a better biscuit. Early in the morning, before anyone could get their face washed and stumble to the table, she had already mixed the biscuit dough from scratch, melted a spoonful of pure butter in a pan she had heated in the oven, and placed the biscuits in the pan, where they baked to a golden brown. She was a perfectionist when it came to her biscuits. If they were just a bit overcooked or charred on the bottom, she was highly critical of the way they appeared. Folks around the table didn't care. With the yellow yolk of farm-fresh eggs dribbling down my chin and the "little round things," as Papa called them, piled high with jam or sorghum, we didn't pay a lot of attention to her self-evaluation. She took so much care and pride in the food she prepared for friends and family. As a bonus, she taught me to pronounce sorghum. I had grown up in Barren County, and my family had always said "sar-gum." Wrong. "Sore-gum," is the correct way, and that's how they say it in Henry County.

Nanny was as magical in the basement canning and putting up tomato juice, jams, and jellies as Papa was out in the garden. In the winter, after the garden was piled high with leaves and other mulch, I headed downstairs. Walking through the basement door, I was greeted by rows and rows of canned goods. Mason jars with Ball caps and lids were stacked from the floor to the ceiling, high above my head. For the trip back home, we stocked up on cardboard boxes filled with canned tomatoes, pear preserves, green beans, and bags of frozen creamed corn. I encouraged her for years to enter her sweet pickles in the State Fair; they were long and green, with a winning taste. There was always room in the car for several jars of pickles. I've never found a store-bought pickle that comes close to Nanny's sweet pickles. It's what God made cucumbers for.

Nanny and Papa were just plain country people. They were kind, helpful to those in need, and famous in the area for cooking up a pot of chili or a chicken casserole and delivering it to anyone housebound. Along with Nanny's incredibly tasty meals, I miss their spirit, their know-how in the garden, and our relationship. Papa passed away several years ago. Nanny is in her 90s and doesn't get out in the garden anymore.

As I write, we live in the city, in a townhouse with little to no backyard. I had considered container gardening, but dismissed it because of our small deck. That, plus the wary eye of our urban neighbors, convinced me to postpone planting until we had a more suitable location, namely, a house with a yard.

The Lexington Farmer's Market is celebrating over 35 years of operation. I've been to Seattle's Pike Place Market, seen rows of flowers and vegetables on display in London and Paris, and shopped at small roadside stands in Georgia and Tennessee. I think the Lexington Farmers' Market is superlative to many other markets I've seen. Most of the vendors move to another location south of the city on Sundays; on Tuesday and Thursday, the market opens downtown near the heart of the city. There are close to a hundred sellers at each location, with a variety of goods and services both expansive and surprising, from a couple selling French crepes and a bicycle-grinding smoothie machine to traditional vegetable, fruit, and flower vendors.

Farmers' market growers and supporters boast about the locally grown products that are usually found only a few miles from the selling location. The growers I've talked with are up early on the day they go to market, packing trucks with produce plucked from the field at the peak of flavor. Many of the fruits and vegetables are grown naturally and organically: hormone-free beef, handmade goat and sheep cheeses, eggs and poultry from free-range fowl, honey, mushrooms, fresh herbs, and spices.

People who visit a farmers' market on a weekly basis have an increased interest in healthier foods, one of the growers told me. Leo Keene owns Blue Moon Farm on the Kentucky River outside Richmond. His specialty is garlic and fresh herbs. He planted his first garlic seedlings in 1988, harvested the next year, and has been growing and selling ever since. Leo is typical of many of the growers. One day as I shopped at the Lexington Farmers' Market, he told me how he got started, how he would get concerned every time he went to the store and found garlic being sold in "coffins"— Styrofoam carton packaging, wrapped in plastic—and knew he could do better. He explained that a garlic bulb is a living thing that doesn't need to be grown, packaged, and transported thousands of miles and sold in a grocery store when it could be cultivated on his own land.

"I plant the seeds in the late fall after the market business has slowed down. By January, in the dead of winter, we have little green shoots, maybe three to five inches tall, sprouting up through the cold ground," he explained as he filled brown paper bags with varieties of garlic and fresh basil. "We also grow a squash medley, 12 to 14 different kinds, and about five to six types of zucchini."

Keene, his wife, and helpers always park their truck and stand in the same place each week, right across from the guitar player who sits on a grassy, shady spot (his tip hat parked conveniently in front of his guitar case). Vendors and musicians alike seem to gravitate to the same areas each week. Keene, a big guy with a wonderful grin and a gray ponytail, also sells fresh goods from the Sunshine Bakery: blackberry muffins, giant cinnamon rolls, whole wheat, raisin and salt-rising breads, and an herb focaccia.

Keene also brokers meats—organically grown lamb, beef and chicken—for a number of farmers in the area who sell to Kentucky restaurants, which helps the bottom line during the year. Keene loves the Saturday market and the camaraderie he has with Blue Moon customers who return each week to his stand.

An amazing array of products greeted me at the market the day I visited. It's more like an outdoor supermarket, with gourmet coffee, Tuscany olive oil, and Dad's Favorite Cheese Spreads; sorghum, honey-pear and red raspberry preserves; and sweet honey straws. There was even a book signing, *Beyond the Fence—A Culinary View of Historic Lexington.* A few feet away, high school students played live jazz. Three Toads Farm had dozens of fresh flowers, including a multitude of daylilies, those rugged, vigorous perennials that come in many colors and shades and sport fascinating names like Ruffled Apricot and Bertie Ferris.

Kate Quarles, who farms and bakes near Waddy, Kentucky, brought 18 different breads to the market: blackberry, carrot-coconut, apple, pineapple-zucchini, strawberry, and pumpkin, to name a few. There was wine from Lovers Leap Winery in Madison County and stand after stand of peaches, cream corn, candy onions, and stringless green beans. The elusive killer tomato was there too, heirloom varieties with the intriguing names of Carmello, the black and purple, and green zebras.

Elmwood Stock Farm would function as a full-service, family grocery on the corner of any street in the county. The farm is owned and operated by a multigenerational Kentucky family that has been farming near Georgetown, Kentucky, for over six generations. Owners Cecil and Kay Bell raise Black Angus cattle and Dorset Suffolk sheep. Cecil's son John and his wife, Melissa, oversee vegetable production. They bring it all to the Lexington Farmers' Market: fresh eggs, beef, poultry, and lamb. On this particular Saturday, they hauled to town seedless grapes, raspberries, new potatoes (harvested in the late spring and early summer), Kennebec potatoes, organic tomatoes, cabbage, and corn. The Bells are there every Saturday, rain or shine.

"I got the idea for grinding a variety of nuts into pure nut butter on a trip to Cape Cod several years ago," Mike Saylers told me. "I was up East on vacation and looking for something a little different to sell, so that and fresh ice cream have put me on the Farmers' Market map."

In a simple machine, which can cost $4000 new, Saylers grinds honey-toasted, organic peanut butter, cashew, and almond butter. The roasted nuts, purchased in Ohio, are dropped in the grinder, a small, plastic cup is placed under the lip of the grinder, and pure, unsweetened, unsalted nut butter pours out. It's much better than store-bought and better for you too.

"I've farmed 170 acres in Franklin County for 28 years and raise watermelons, asparagus and hogs, corn for grain, and pasture grass for hay," Saylers added. "I have a fellow in Bowling Green that makes about 10 different flavors of ice cream, and along with pork and chicken-barbeque sandwiches, I can make a living," he said. Saylers always has a big grin and friendly greeting for anyone wandering past his stand.

People visit the Lexington Farmers' Market for many reasons, but I firmly believe it is the tomato that draws hundreds to Cheapside Park each Saturday. Mike's peanut butter is better than any store brand, the breads and jams are tasty, the young Italian men selling fresh pasta are unique, but it's the tomato that beckons.

Visit any seed store, hang around the gardening section at Home Depot, or talk to an experienced neighbor who nails the killer tomato every growing season, and you hear tomato stories. I've always enjoyed talking with gardeners about successful tomato-growing methods or investigating the right and wrong ways to go about mounding and cupping the dirt around the plant to hold in moisture. I wonder if it's better to stake tomatoes to tobacco sticks using old pantyhose or to let them run on the ground. I've had my soil tested by the county extension agent to gauge the pH. Based on that, I've added lime to the garden to balance the soil.

I've studied mulch. Egg shells and leftovers? Leaves and animal manure? (Though no more Patty-cakes from the circus.) I've spent the winter indoors, measuring, laying out the plot, sketching and labeling where everything might be planted. I've gotten bogged down in the details and longed for the first warm days of spring— only to wait six more weeks.

The U.S. Department of Agriculture reports that tomatoes are the most popular home-grown vegetable in America. Some asparagus and corn fanatics might argue that point. But given the astonishingly delicious flavor of a well-grown, mature tomato, especially compared to the insipid ones in the grocery aisles, the tomato wins, no contest.

Consider, too, the health benefits. Tomatoes are not just good, they're good for you. In recent years, studies have shown that tomatoes are a rich source of lycopene, a chemical that gives tomatoes, strawberries, and carrots their distinctive colors. A number of studies suggest that lycopene helps prevent several types of cancer. Try throwing that into a conversation at the Home Depot.

We're in the process of relocating from an urban condo to a

small house near downtown. A house with a yard, a garden plot, a place to once again grow the killer tomato. I'm going back to the basics—sunny spot, near water. That's it. Let nature take its course.

Grow, prize tomato, grow. Do your thing. You're on your own. Good luck.

I'll be nearby with the watering can if you need me. And if you think you might need a visit from a certain circus elephant I know...

To Beat or Not to Beat...a Biscuit

Years before the Food Network realized that Bobby Flay's *Barbecue Addiction* and *Giada at Home* could become immensely popular television and magazine franchises, I thought my mother was the "Queen of Southern Cuisine." She would have given the drippy drawl of today's Southern kitchen maven, Paula Deen, a run for her money. My mother was a sensational chef. Er, make that cook.

My mother served up mouth-watering crispy fried chicken long before the Colonel's drive-thru window became a popular dinner-time destination. She made juicy meatloaf filled with just the right amount of bread crumbs and bits of celery, topped with a garnish of tomato sauce, coupled with homemade yeast rolls that melted in your mouth and pork chops so tender you could cut them with a fork.

Occasionally, there were dishes fixed just for my hard-working daddy, who spent 14 hours on the road working—liver and onions, calf brains and eggs, cheese grits and kale, none of which ranked up there on my list of all-time favorite dishes from Mom.

She wasn't a fancy cook, although she and my dad enjoyed watching Julia Child on their first black-and-white television set in the 1950s. They also adored Graham Kerr, "the Galloping Gourmet." I don't believe Mom ever attempted a frilly French soufflé, and my dad was strictly a meat-and-potatoes man. Yet he would come home for lunch just in time to watch Kerr's noon network show with her. I think they both fancied his British accent.

My sister told me Mom had quite a reputation in our small Barren County, Kentucky hometown for Benedictine spread, the cream-cheese concoction that turned green when cucumber and food coloring were added. She painted it on triangles of pink-and-lime-colored bread with the crusts removed. Mom always whipped it up when she was having bridge club or for one of my sister's little-girl parties. Dad and I preferred our cheese American-style. If I was going to eat a cucumber, I wanted it in the form of a pickle—a slice or two of dill or one of those whale-size whole pickle spears you had to stab with a fork out of a jar at the drive-in concession stand.

I don't ever remember asking my mother how she learned to cook. I believe she was self-taught. Neither of my grandmothers was very talented in the kitchen, so Mom didn't pick up many tips from them.

If you were fortunate enough to have a stay-at-home mom in the 1950s, you might have had a breakfast of bacon, eggs, and toast waiting for you as you wiped the sleepies out of your eyes. On weekends, you got pancakes or homemade waffles with maple syrup. If you were home from school at lunchtime, your mom might have served fresh tuna fish salad or a fried bologna sandwich. (The secret to this delicacy was making a few cuts in the edge of the bologna circle to prevent the slice from curling up into a shallow bowl as it cooked.) After school, you might have been treated to a steaming cup of hot chocolate and freshly baked Toll House cookies or S'mores, gooey and soft after a quick trip in the oven. During the evening, you might have finished a vigorous three-on-three basketball game with the neighborhood boys just when your mom blew the dog whistle to call you home to a mound of mashed potatoes, green beans, minute steak, and cornbread.

Nobody made a fuss over all this or asked Mom for a recipe. I'm not even sure we ever thanked her enough for taking care of us and preparing such tasty yet simple meals and after-school treats.

But I sure do miss them.

Sunday lunches were always unique, with their own exclusive menus. We'd all been to Sunday School and church and, unlike the meals at suppertime during the week when my father didn't always make it home to eat with the family, we all sat down at our "breakfast room" table together— my little sister, my big sister (if she was at home from college or a job), Mom, Dad, and me. Mom took a few minutes to mix her homemade chicken salad or a fresh fruit and Jell-O salad. We looked forward to a divinely baked pecan pie, luscious lemon icebox pie, or homemade brownies with vanilla ice cream drizzled with chocolate sauce.

Even today, an almost Pavlovian response is triggered in me when Sundays, lunchtime, and church are all mentioned in the same breath. It conjures up thoughts of family, food, and beaten biscuits. When I mention beaten biscuits in conversation, most people ask: "What's a beaten biscuit?"

Beaten biscuits are a firm, dry biscuit, with a texture halfway between that of a risen baking-powder biscuit and a soda cracker. I've found that people are surprised when they first have one. They expect a soft baking-powder biscuit. Instead, the composition is unique: crisp, flaky, and chewy all at the same time.

Beaten biscuits originated in Virginia, and traveled north to Maryland and across the mountains to Kentucky in the early 1800s. They were present in many upper-class homes. Apparently, the mistress of the house liked having these biscuits on hand at all times. They were a status symbol that showed you had "help" who made them for you. In the 1800s, it was quite a process to make them from scratch: mix flour, a little lard, milk—and then beat the tar out of the mixture.

The dough eventually becomes smooth and "blistered" from the beating—bubbles of air start to pop out. Food historians have written that the beating process could take 30 minutes and requires as many as three hundred to five hundred whacks with a mallet or rolling pin. When done, the dough is rolled out and cut into rounds, or formed by hand into smooth shapes slightly larger than a 50-cent piece, pierced with a fork, and baked on baking sheets.

My mother made hers with a gadget known as a biscuit brake. She would fold the dough and pass it through the apparatus. A food processor would be used now. My daddy loved them with slivers of country ham; I smeared them with real butter. We have them at Thanksgiving now. My little sister asks me to bring them to the table every year. But when we were growing up, beaten biscuits were a Sunday ritual: chicken salad and beaten biscuits—*only* on Sundays. Mom didn't serve them during the week.

Today, I wish I could ask her why.

When I was a boy growing up in our small town of Glasgow in south central Kentucky, I remember the Baptist Church looming large over our community. At the corner of South Green and College Streets, it was one of the largest buildings in the city, dwarfed only by the courthouse on the square a few blocks north. Anyone living on the south side of town always referenced it when giving directions to the north side of the city: "Well, you just go up South Green about a half-mile, just past the big Baptist Church before you get to the square, and keep on going round the square till you get to the red light, and then take a right on Race." It didn't matter that the First Methodist Church was on the right or that St. Helen's, the only Catholic Church in town, was on the left. The Baptist Church was always used as the landmark.

The church occupied an entire block. Except for the George J. Ellis drugstore, Richardson Hardware, the pool hall, and the National Stores on the square where my grandmother worked, the Baptist Church was the closest thing to the center of the universe for a boy growing up in that place and time.

Right across the street from the church was Shorty's DX Service Station. Pig, a bull of a man with a bulbous nose, worked there and could fix a flat tire on a bicycle, pump gas, clean a front windshield, and make change all at the same time. We often bought Bazooka bubblegum by the piece out of a big jar that Shorty kept next to the cash register. Right across the street from Shorty's was the Hill Service Station, which I didn't frequent much because they seemed to cater more to the farmers and heavy-equipment operators and didn't have time for a kid with a flat tire on his bike.

But Sundays at Hill Service were different. They had a row of vending machines outside the front door, and most Sundays, weather permitting, we'd take a break between Sunday school and church and dash across the street for a Coke and some peanuts. There was always time to pop open the bottle of Coke, pour a nickel bag of salted nuts into the neck of the bottle, and talk about what time we were going to meet later for our Sunday afternoon game of baseball.

Across the street from Hill Service, headed toward the square, was our family's doctor's office, the brothers John and Lewis Dickenson. Next to them was my favorite building in town, the Mary Wood Weldon Public Library, and farther up the street was the Glasgow elementary, junior, and high school complex of buildings. Before you got to the school, you passed J&H Market, the only grocery store on that side of town.

So, you could get an education, religion, a book, a homemade chicken-salad sandwich, a Coke, a clean windshield, and a piece of

Bazooka bubblegum all within a stone's throw of each other. Life was grand.

My father used the Glasgow Baptist Church as a reference point when directing salesmen or delivery trucks to his company. His wholesale distributing business had been on the College Street location for nearly 20 years, but there were still out-of-towners who needed a guidepost to direct them to his store.

Dad loved working. He loved working so much he did it six-and-a-half days a week. He loved working so much he would stay at the store on Christmas Eve (unless that day fell on Sunday) until four or five o'clock in the afternoon. Many nights he would finish up, come home for a warmed-up supper, and head back to the store to help the Gordon potato chip man unload and stack cases of product in the warehouse. There were eight to 10 employees he could have called to unload, but he did it himself rather than disturbing them at home. He was just like that. He started the company in the middle of the Depression and toiled like that all of his life. I don't think he knew any other way.

Even when business began to pick up 20 years after the Depression, he didn't change his work habits. When the men he had grown up with locked the doors of their businesses on Friday afternoon so they could play golf all day on Saturday, Dad stayed at the store. When his buddies invited him to make the two-and-a-half hour drive to Cincinnati to take in a Reds game, he politely begged off. He made deliveries to restaurants or stores that ran short for the weekend or worked on the books. In a way, it was kind of sad. But he was a happy man.

The half-day my father didn't work, Sunday morning, belonged to the Lord.

Born and raised in Barren County, he had been a member of the Glasgow Baptist Church all of his life and, although not a religious zealot, he was a devoted and loyal church member. Deacon, pastor search committee member, Sunday school teacher, Wednesday evening prayer service leader and once or twice a year, when he could rush through his out-of-town sales route and get back to the pew for the visiting evangelist, revival attendee. As a youngster, I recall being proud of his position in the church, his ability to lead the Sunday offering prayer, or deliver the invocation.

Dad's Sunday morning schedule included my sister and me. It took on the aspect of a ritual in its regularity: Wake up, have pancakes or French toast prepared by Mother, bathe, dress (pants pressed, tie and jacket, polished Sunday shoes), and into Dad's front seat for the short trip up the street to church. With a click of the radio, the dulcet tones of the Blackwood Brothers and the Happy Goodman Family gospel radio hour would fill the car. We were off, but not before a requisite stop at the post office mailbox to pick up important invoices and checks that Dad would work on later that day. Only after that, with the radio blaring "What A Friend We Have in Jesus," did we arrive at Sunday school.

When my sister and I were in grade school, we learned our early religion and belief system from him. Our mother attended the First Christian Disciples of Christ Church, located near the post office on the Glasgow square. My grandmother played the organ, but we rarely attended services there. (Mom and Dad must have had an arrangement regarding the denomination their children would be raised in.) Later, it was what we were taught in Sunday school, Baptist Training Union (BTU) and vacation Bible school that nurtured us in our formative church years. There were hours of Bible recitation and Bible verse competition; perfect attendance pins and certificates for accomplishment in Biblical knowledge; cherry Kool-Aid and vanilla wafers for memorization of a favorite Bible scripture.

I remember an evening my father took the time to have the "come to Jesus" talk with me in my bedroom. The church revival was being conducted, and the Reverend Van Eaton, a tower of a man with a powerful, booming voice, was the visiting evangelist. All of the eight, nine and ten-year-olds had been to Sunday school and church together for years. My cousins, our friends and others had been given limited, but nevertheless important lessons in what it meant to give your life to Christ.

All of the boys marched to the front of the congregation where we were met with the furrowed brow and deep voice of Reverend Eaton. He strolled slowly by each of us, whispering a few "God bless you's" in each ear. His big hand started at your shoulder and slowly moved to just above the elbow when he asked, "Do you believe in the Lord Jesus Christ as your personal savior, and do you believe that Jesus can forgive your sins?'"

Huge issues for an eight-year-old to grapple with in just a few seconds, but I had enough sense to realize it beat the alternative. I had read about Hell, dreamed about it, and asked questions about how hot it could really get. I had been told it was the dropping-off place for all sinners who didn't correctly answer the question being asked in front of the congregation on that Wednesday evening revival service. The Baptist Church of my childhood was paramount to my growing up in Glasgow.

After church on warm spring and summer days, I pulled off my clip-on tie and walked the mile or so home. South Green Street was lined with roomy houses adorned with white columns and spacious front porches. I ambled toward my home at 109 Norris Court, waving to the folks who were kind enough to honk their car horns at me, but who didn't bother to offer me a ride home. They knew where I was going. They knew I would arrive safe and that I was working up an appetite for Sunday lunch with Mom, Dad, my sister—and a plate of chicken salad and beaten biscuits.

On Finding a Family and a Dog

September 2010

Tally-Ho Burton stood in the center of a small circle, surrounded by family members who reached out to gently stroke the thick hair that covered his back. His shiny coat caught the light from flash cameras as excited members of the Trigg clan snapped pictures, eagerly touching his muscular rib cage that slimmed to a narrow waist. My five-year-old granddaughter's tiny hand brushed the foxhound's broad forehead, and she quickly gave him a careful hug. "Look Grandy," she exclaimed, "he likes me!"

The foxhound who so proudly and symbolically stood before us that early-fall evening in Barren County, Kentucky, was only one of the highlights and discoveries made on the weekend of the first-ever Trigg family reunion in modern times.

My mother's maiden name was Trigg. She was born and raised in South Central Kentucky with an older sister and two younger brothers. My younger sister's first name is Trigg. My older sister, Charlotte, was named for my mother's sister, who died in childhood in 1918. We were familiar with the Trigg name and family. Our childhood was punctuated by visits to Trigg family uncles and aunts and their children who lived in Florida. They, too, came to Kentucky a few days every other summer.

But, other than a story here and there, we knew very little about the Trigg ancestry. On my father's side, there was a Goodman family reunion every year on the third Sunday in May. We always looked forward to it because it meant our worshiping was limited to Sunday school. We were too busy stocking the car with crispy fried chicken, home-cooked, garden-fresh green beans and a two-layer chocolate cake or two. Once the car was loaded we drove to Fountain Run, a tiny town with a population of 260 in Monroe County near where Allen, Monroe, and Barren Counties come together. Fountain Run was the home of the Goodmans. We never missed a third Sunday in May when I was a child.

That was my father's side of the family. On my mother's side, we had never had a family reunion until September 2010 when a group of us got together. We all had questions—and not many answers—about relatives who were rumored to have fought in the Revolutionary War, battled Indians with Daniel Boone, or had learned the banking business to find success during the 1920s, only to go bankrupt during the Depression.

My cousin Lance Trigg and I had discussed this first reunion for two years before it took place. In anticipation of all of us getting together, my niece Beth had waded knee-deep through Ancestry.com, preparing profiles of several long-lost relatives. In search of family treasure, each of us had plowed through closets and piles of tattered, faded, black-and-white photos. The word went out over email to relatives in Michigan, Texas, Florida, North Carolina, Georgia, Tennessee, and Kentucky. The surviving matriarch, 84-year-old Helen Trigg, who had married my mother's brother 60 years ago, made the trip from her home in Florida.

On the first evening of the reunion, as family members began to arrive, we dug into boxes of photos like greedy children. A Trigg family crest pin was handed out to everyone in attendance and worn with pride. My niece Beth, who had taken the time to do the most extensive genealogical research, taped a carefully constructed and detailed family tree on the wall of the cabin. The highlight of the night was the arrival of the foxhound, who was as much a part of the family as any of us who had made the trip to the reunion.

Foxhunting

The history of foxhunting, a vigorous sport in Britain, Ireland, and later America, can be traced to prehistoric man and through the ancient and medieval hunting practice of wild game for sport. Before 1500 BC, the Egyptians hunted on foot with scenting hounds, greyhounds, big fighting dogs, and small dogs like terriers used for rabbit hunting. The hounds in ancient Greece were described as a cross between a dog and a fox. A good hound had a good nose, long ears, cat-like feet, strength, speed, and agility. A good pack hunted together, noses close and maintaining a steady pace.

In England, during the period 1750-1800, the development of

hounds changed, with increased speed and drive. Good hounds had a breadth of breast, depth of chest, a well-developed rib cage, sloping shoulders, muscled forearms, and strong quarters for running and jumping. Foxhunting was taken to the New World by English colonists; there is evidence that as early as 1607 in Jamestown and in the tidewater region of Virginia, countrymen were keeping three or four mongrel dogs at a time to destroy vermin, as well as wolves, raccoons, and foxes.

In the 1800s, it was apparent that American attitudes toward foxhunting varied enormously. In the South, it represented a more social, genteel activity where the sport of the chase developed around hunting clubs (which eventually evolved into modern-day golf country clubs). Members' horses were stabled at the club; the hunters slept in club bedrooms and drank at club bars; the hunt was a club function. The "correct costume," consisting of properly cut scarlet coats, velvet caps, high boots, and buckskin gloves, was essential in the hunting field.

Ancestors of American foxhounds, like Tally-Ho Burton, who stood in the lake cabin before us and was a descendant of the first Trigg-bred dog, were being born and bred in the 1800s. Colonel Haiden C. Trigg raised foxhounds for 25 years, beginning in 1866. According to author Roger Longrigg's *History of Foxhunting*, Colonel Trigg is quoted as saying, "I owned a pack of those long-eared, rat-tail, deep-toned, black and tan Virginia foxhounds. In those happy bygone days I could, on a moonlight night, ride to the covert-side, throw my leg over the saddle and listen for hours to the most magnificent music made by the ever-to-be-remembered dogs. The red fox came." It was then that my great-grandfather began buying a few hounds, and from those, bred the Trigg Red Fox dog.

The Trigg foxhound had been bred as a superior hunting dog over a hundred years ago and is still very much a part of the sport of foxhunting today. Haiden Curd Trigg was born in Barren County in 1834, on the farm where we had discovered the family cemetery. He was the grandson of a gentleman who was instrumental in the settlement of Glasgow and Barren County. Known as Colonel Trigg, he was a businessman involved in the railroad industry, among other enterprises.

An article in the Glasgow newspaper, which might have been

an obituary written and printed when he died at 77, told more. He attended school in Barren County and Urania College, located in Glasgow. Trigg had worked in Louisville in the hardware business, but returned to his hometown to establish a bank. He founded a second bank and was president of the Glasgow Railroad Company. Obituaries and profiles of the time were written in a newspaper style that isn't recognized today. His obituary was accompanied by a remarkably clear photograph of him sitting in what appears to be an ornately decorated rocking chair, wearing a dark waistcoat, wide tie and white-collared dress shirt popular at the period. The sharp features of his face—stern, serious, unsmiling—were surrounded by a neatly trimmed white beard.

The writer wrote: "In his political affiliations, Mr. Trigg is a staunch advocate of the principles and policies for which the Democratic Party stands sponsor. He has never aspired to public office of any description, but is ever ready to give of his aid and influence in support of all measures and enterprises advanced for the progress and development of this section of the state. While not formally connected with any religious organization, he is nevertheless a Christian man—of a large heart and great benevolence. In his home he has a 'Prophet's Chamber' where ministers and other good men are frequently entertained."

The article also mentioned that "although advanced in years, Haiden C. Trigg still retains, in much of their pristine vigor, the splendid mental and physical qualities of his youth. This is due in large measure to the fact that he is a natural born sportsman, one who is fond of all kinds of healthy out-of-door exercise, his one big hobby being the chase."

For more on Trigg's passion for "the chase" and his enthusiasm for breeding an exceptional dog, which had cemented his reputation in the hunting world, I turned once again to Beth, who was quickly becoming the go-to genealogist in the family.

I called her one night from my home in Kentucky, reaching her in North Carolina, where she had moved several years ago.

"I'm doing some work on Haiden C. Trigg and need some info on the dogs, breeding, and the sport," I began.

Without hesitating, Beth gave a quick reply. "Why don't you get a copy of his book?"

Businessman, banker, breeder, and author Haiden Trigg had written *The American Foxhound* in 1890. According to the preface, Trigg had intended the volume to be a brief history of the origins of the Trigg, Birdsong, and Maupin strains of the Trigg Red Fox dog. He wrote that after working and breeding the dogs for 25 years, discussing their skill, and reading correspondence verifying their prowess from others across the United States, he felt confident "that we have a strain of dogs at least as good as those of their famous ancestors—we know from almost daily experience that we can run to earth or catch the red fox."

The compendium is replete with descriptions of fox hunts, correspondence from breeders written in the middle to late 1800s, and breeding lineage of the most famous dogs. There is even a touch of national pride, pitting the Trigg dog against the English-bred hound.

My relative wrote: "The English people, for centuries, have indulged in the fox chase and have spent thousands of pounds for the improvement of the hound. We think our best strains of dogs today are equal, if not superior, to the English, for this country. This, we know, is a bold assertion, and may be challenged, but 'tis said, experience is the best of teachers."

At our fall reunion, a Bowling Green dog breeder had brought Tally-Ho Burton, a full-blooded, Trigg foxhound, to show the family. The hound matched the description of the dogs I'd read about, but Tally-Ho Burton was much burlier and thicker than I had imagined. Not short and squatty like a beagle, but tall, about two feet high with long, muscular legs and wide feet. He was black and white with a tan blanketed back. He was built for speed: he had a large rib cage that slimmed to a narrow waist and a bushy tail he carried gracefully over his back. He seemed gentle and enjoyed the attention he was receiving from the family who shared his name.

My great-grandfather was very aware that the breed needed a strong, deep, loud voice: a normal bark followed by a high pitch howl. He bred the Trigg hound to sound like a freight train barreling through the forest.

At the reunion, in the midst of the family celebration, the laughter of grandchildren, the exchange of photographs and memorabilia, I found myself staring at the Trigg dog. Was this the connection to our past we had all yearned for? Was Tally-Ho Burton and the blood that coursed through his strong yet agile body descended from the same DNA that Haiden Trigg had bred into those first dogs, Forest, Rip, and Fannie?

In *The American Foxhound*, my great-grandfather wrote a remarkable introductory text on purchasing, breeding, and raising a foxhound. According to Trigg, the American foxhound needed to be bred differently than the hounds found in England, with one distinguishing factor—a superior nose and the ability to roam longer distances. He points out that the English hound of the same speed in an open area, might be "out-footed" by the smaller American dog in the briar-fields and heavy undergrowth of the American forests. As a master gardener might teach a budding group of backyard horticulturists, Trigg became a mentor to those who longed to know how to best ensure the dog's other admirable qualities—a good nose, good tongue, looks pleasing to the eye, and uniform in size and color.

He realized the importance of the care and feeding of puppies to be sure they grew into the strong foxhounds. He recommended feeding them regularly on "wholesome food—a puppy fed entirely on meat, or the refuse of a slaughter-pen, will develop an abnormal neck and head and become awkward in his actions." There is more advice on the patience the owner must possess to raise a good pack. He suggested owners practice a modicum of silence when beginning a hunt—"Learn to keep your mouth shut," he warned, so the fox would not get a head start on the dogs.

Great-grandfather Haiden writes this tale to close out the first chapter, a final admonishment from the master of the hounds to his northern brethren interested in purchasing the dogs being bred in the Commonwealth:

"A few years ago we received a letter from a gentleman north of Ohio, who claims to be a great lover of the chase and advertises his strain of dogs extensively. In replying to him, we made the inquiry as to his mode of hunting, whether his country was a good one to ride over, and did he have horses that were trained to take fences. Replying to our inquiry, he said that he 'usually hunted in a buggy.' We dropped his letter in the waste-basket and never replied."

Oh, those damn Yankees!

Today there is still an active National Trigg Foxhunter's Association with show records spanning more than a hundred years.

Learning about the Trigg dog was only part of our discovery process. Reading and discussing the various histories and collections of material that had been amassed at this first reunion, we explored the past like eager students contemplating a complicated calculus equation. For example, we learned of our Norse and Viking heritage, how the Triggs could be found in the first Jamestown Colony; our role in The War of 1812; and that our ancestors wore the Southern gray of the Confederacy during the Civil War. Among them were men and women with strong names: Daniel, Abraham, Sussannah, and William. They were bankers, farmers, and businessmen. One of the females, Louise Trigg, was trained as a doctor in Philadelphia and returned to Kentucky to practice. They were accomplished musicians, playing in orchestras and teaching piano, cello, and violin to school children and adults. One of the several Triggs named Haiden had served in the Kentucky House of Representatives; another was the first Justice of the Peace in Barren County in 1798, six years after Kentucky became a state.

On a visit to the Barren County Cultural Center and Museum, we learned William F. Trigg was an early 1800s distiller and a horse trader, and that A. Trigg had driven large droves of hogs to Richmond, Virginia, for slaughter. The first cotton gin in the county had been erected by a Trigg. We read from an early recorded history of Alanson Trigg, a colorful character who had owned a thousand-acre farm three miles south of Glasgow in the years before the Civil War. He was described as being over six feet tall with an Adam's apple that was more noticeable because it worked up and down the more excited he became in conversation, and that nearly always occurred when money was mentioned. To add to his distinctive physical features, he was one-eyed. A barnyard chicken had pecked his eye out of his head when he was a small boy. It was also written that "he owned a big lot of Negroes" and farmed a great amount of acreage.

Perhaps of all the wondrous and curious details we learned during this first Trigg reunion, the most wondrous and curious of all was uncovering the secret of the lost cemetery. In various documents, we found references to a farm where many of our relatives had lived in the 19th century. My sisters and I weren't aware of its existence. With the help of the director of the county museum, we learned of the farm's location, about three miles south of Glasgow. When we arrived, a woman was getting ready to start her mower. I approached and asked if she could point us to the cemetery. She led us past a barn, through a middle of September-harvested cornfield, to an isolated clump of brush and fallen trees in the middle of the field. Someone at the museum had mentioned "tall cedar trees" as a clue to finding the site, and true to that description, a glade of cedars towered above cracked and broken headstones. We struggled through thorny vines, poison ivy, and fallen timber to get past a rusty iron gate and fence. There we spotted the first grave marker:

Alanson M. Trigg, January 08, 1795-May 12, 1873

After a quiet second or two, Beth broke the silence. "Alanson was Granny's great-grandfather."

Pulling away the debris and fallen limbs, we discovered more tombstones: Mary, born 1830, died 1865; Thomas, born 1845, died 1860; a son, Alanson, born 1830, died 1863. Family records told us there was supposed to be seven in all, although we didn't find that many. The Trigg headstones were elaborately carved and lettered. A few plain, undated markers confused us. Eventually, we decided they might have been the graves of slaves buried beside their master, but that was pure guesswork on our part. Still, the startling thought of our family "owning" slaves gave us pause as we traipsed through the undergrowth.

We searched through the small overgrown oasis of our heritage for a few more minutes, then climbed back over the iron fence and were on our way. Later, the 20 or so family members who made the trip to Kentucky and Barren County planned to return to the cemetery for a cleanup project.

In the evening, we gathered on a cabin porch before dinner and listened intently as Beth told us of one of the prominent Trigg women. After posing for a group photo, we quietly reflected on what the reunion had meant to us. I mentioned I was curious to understand why it took us so long to gather as a family. No one had a good answer. Some of the family members had moved far away; others didn't have an interest in the past. Whatever the reasons, we overcame them and vowed to keep the Trigg family reunion alive for years to come.

October 2011

The brown speckled toad scampered quickly under leaves and fallen branches scattered throughout the small Trigg family cemetery. We were disturbing his home in our quest to unearth fallen tombstones and rid the plot of dead trees, poison ivy, barbed wire, and an iron gate and fence that once surrounded the place. In places, the gate was twisted in the ground like a pretzel, buried under years of dirt and debris; the gate, bent from the weight of a fallen oak, needed replacing. We were standing in the middle of a cornfield in the only acreage not planted and harvested that fall by the farmer who leases the land from the current owner. He had given us access to the property—land that once belonged to our family. We dubbed our amphibious visitor the "Trigg Toad" and promised to return him to his "mansion" later in the day.

"Let me pull the truck right through here, and we'll find a sinkhole to dump everything in," Lance, my cousin, pronounced, quickly taking the helm as captain of the cleanup. Frankly, I was surprised we were once again standing in the cornfield, three miles from the heart of Glasgow, Kentucky, staring what at appeared to be an insurmountable mountain of overgrown vines and fallen trees. We had come back to Barren County to cut, clean, and restore the Trigg family cemetery to a presentable state. It was going to be quite a task.

Beth's sleuthing found records indicating seven members of the Trigg family should have been buried in the plot. Our objective on this bright, crisp fall day was to simply identify the tombstones, straighten them up, and tidy the plot.

In the year since we'd been on the property, the dense growth of thorny bushes, brambles, and briars appeared to have experienced a bumper year. Lance arrived, driving a huge Chevy Suburban, pulling a trailer stocked with every imaginable gas-powered and hand tool he could haul from his home in Florida.

"Come on over here, and let's talk about our plan of attack," Lance shouted. "I suggest we divide up, attack it from the outside, cut a clearing so someone can get in there to the graves, and work our way toward the center." It sounded like instructions for a military operation. He unlatched the trailer door and pulled back a tarpaulin. I had brought a rake and a pair of gloves. Lance's trailer was packed with clearing saws, pruning shears, weed eaters, string trimmers, and a couple of axes and hatchets. Toward the front of the flatbed was a monstrous brush cutter whose collapsed handle had kept it hidden from view.

"We'll use that to cut the ring of saplings and scrub trees surrounding the perimeter," Lance said. When I saw this piece of gear in action I knew why he had brought it: with its wide, flat front, housing a variety of sharp blades, the operator could drive it like a lawnmower, through, over, and in between anything in its path. It snapped off seedlings and young trees like they were blades of grass.

From under the trailer's tarp, we pulled machetes, hoes, shovels, small digging tools, and an array of other equipment and tossed them on the ground. Then Lance demonstrated the hydraulic lift. His plan was to pile the trailer full, drive it to the edge of the field, find a low point or sinkhole, and dump the load. It lifted just like the toy dump trucks I had as a kid. I looked at my wife, Debbie, and whispered, "Whoa, he's serious about this."

By mid-morning, an early-dawn mist had lifted. An autumn sun announced a nearly perfect day for the work ahead. A small canopy was erected for shade. Water, Gatorade, and soft drinks were available, and my sister Trigg soon left for the lunch run.

My son Will, an anthropologist with the University of Kentucky, whose job it was to survey cemeteries like this one all over Kentucky, had volunteered his professional services. He suggested the plot needed to be mapped—measure the circumference, draw plot lines, graph the location of the graves we could identify—being careful not to disturb anything during this process.

State law prohibits the disruption of cemeteries, even for

cleanup, Will even suggested that the overturned tombstones be left on the ground and not straightened up until we knew more about what the law allowed us to do.

I've learned that Kentucky cemeteries and graveyards face dramatic pressures—from development, from abandonment and decay, from nature, like the huge tree that had fallen across several of our Trigg tombstones, and from vandals. The graveyard plot itself, the original deed, and the legal complexities of the cemetery being located on private property all sent me scurrying to state experts and national Web sites for guidance. Since the discovery of the lost family cemetery, I'll admit to a feeling of wanting to save the graveyard and get to work on it immediately. This may have been a mistake. A preservationist at the Kentucky Historical Society advised that when preservation efforts are rushed, the potential exists for serious and long-lasting damage. Our family needed to investigate a wide range of disciplines, including the original landscape architecture, the ongoing historical research confirming grave identification, and the difference between preserving and restoring many of the head and footstones. I needed to be the catalyst in developing a long-range plan for preserving what our forefathers had left us.

At noon, we took a break for sandwiches. Lance and his brother Steve, an orthopedist practicing in Jacksonville, Florida, had made a dozen trips to the edge of the field to dump trailer loads of vines, trees, and stumps from downed trees. A giant oak tree had fallen into the cemetery; its massive girth measuring three to five feet in diameter. It had fallen across a tombstone and had to be removed. After hours of work with chainsaws, the oak was divided into sizable bites and hauled away. Underneath were the grave and headstone:

Price G. Trigg, 23 March, 1844-20 February, 1852

Beth's records confirmed he had died at age seven.

Will had plotted the small gravesites and had mapped Alanson's tombstone at the far left, westward side of the cemetery, but facing east. This is where we found his head and footstone. As was the custom, the patriarch of a family was buried at what was considered the head or top of the grave plot and always facing east. All of the other burial sites were in rows, also facing east: Eliza Jane; Mary Ann; a son, Alanson, who died at age 32 and never married; Thomas H., who had passed at age 14. Beth's investigation also revealed that some of the children and a second wife might have been laid to rest in the Glasgow city cemetery. We couldn't answer why.

But we think we may have solved the mystery of the small stones we had originally thought might belong to slaves. They didn't. Some graves in the 18th century contained footstones to demarcate the foot end of the grave. These stones sometimes developed into full curb sets marking the entire perimeter of the grave. Footstones were rarely annotated with more than the deceased's initials and year of death, and sometimes a memorial mason and plot reference number. Many cemeteries and churchyards removed footstones to ease grass cutting. The location of these stones, not more than a foot in circumference, six inches or so wide, helped us find the burial sites. Some of the head and footstones were completely covered with vines and dirt and had to be excavated in order to read who they belonged to.

At the end of a long day, with the sun playing hide and seek across a glorious Kentucky sky and billowing clouds just beginning to cast shadows on the Trigg cemetery, we decided we'd had enough. Our family cemetery had undergone a miraculous transformation in just one day: from overgrown and abandoned to more presentable as a burial site, rid of the poison ivy and fallen oak tree. The cedar trees remain. Some live for hundreds of years. Because of a lightning strike and fire, one of the cedars had to be removed. And, as the chainsaw gang cut their way through the stump, each family member was presented with a slice of the cedar that might have been there when Alanson Munson Trigg buried members of his family in the family plot, and where he too was laid to rest in 1873.

My father, Henry Goodman

My mother, in her kitchen in Glasgow

Our home at 109 Norris Court, Glasgow

Mom and Dad in the living room of our Glasgow home

My big sister Charlotte, little sister Trigg and me in front of our
Glasgow home

Mom and Dad and one of their first automobiles

Me, in front of our house on Washington St. in Glasgow, where I
lived until age 5

Mom in her kitchen

Dad even wore a tie on a weekend state park trip!

Mom bakes a birthday cake

Joseph Dudley Downing:
Poet of Color and Light

We had talked about what he might wear to the family reunion. My seven-year-old sister and I, at 10, had seen a picture of him. He was wearing what looked to me like a dress or nightshirt, similar to the one the father wore in the illustrations of *The Night Before Christmas.* In the photograph from *Time* magazine, he wore what appeared to be a wide-brimmed ladies' hat with a dark band around the center. My mother said his dress was more like a floor-length cotton robe. She said artists in France dressed that way, and she added, "Besides, your cousin Dudley is flamboyant; he has a certain flair about him."

We looked over for a nod of confirmation from my dad, who was driving the car loaded with a couple of lawn chairs and the picnic supplies we needed for the Goodman family reunion in Fountain Run, Kentucky. He murmured, "Uh-huh, your mother knows how they dress in France."

It was 1956, and every fourth Sunday in May since I could remember, and many fourth Sundays before that, the Goodman's gathered for a family reunion in Monroe County at a small cemetery where our forefathers rested, near the Tennessee border. For generations, this land had been celebrated as our "home place." A couple of miles down the road from the cemetery was a dilapidated farmhouse where our great-great grandfather had fathered 32 children. He was probably the most famous relative in the family until we learned more about our cousin Dudley, who was coming all the way from France and promised to be the highlight of this year's celebration.

My mother had filled a platter with fried chicken, covered two-dozen deviled eggs with aluminum foil to keep them fresh, cooked enough spuds for a bowl of potato salad, and made sweet tea and Kool-Aid to keep our thirst at bay during the hottest portion of the day. With the windows rolled down to let in the late May breeze,

I settled into a corner of the backseat as we drove past Barren River Lake onto curvy Highway 87, the two-lane road that took us through the minuscule hamlets of Austin and Tracy. I daydreamed about the day ahead: picnic on the grounds, an afternoon baseball game across the road from the cemetery with my cousins, and a renewal of the family's relationship with our artist cousin from France.

Cousin Dudley wasn't wearing a dress. When we arrived in the late morning, he was surrounded by adoring family members, brothers Dero and George at his elbow, sister Sara close by. Dud was wearing dull, yellowish-tan trousers and a guayabera shirt. It could have been a khaki uniform if not for the accessories. A thin, brilliant-orange scarf was tied around his neck, knotted just below the Adam's apple. He wore a patchwork sleeveless vest adorned with small brass buttons. Around his neck, several strands of leather; from one hung an Indian arrowhead. He wore glasses and had graying hair.

My dad and most of the other men were dressed in their Sunday best, including neckties they had yet to take off in the early-summer sun. My dad kept his on all afternoon, so there was a noticeable contrast in how our European visitor was dressed. I felt a bit self-conscious in my short pants. At least "Little D," another cousin, had worn long pants. A couple of people shuffled out of the way, giving my sister and me a chance to scoot in a little closer, be introduced, and shake Dud's hand.

That's when I noticed his feet. He wore sandals—with no socks.

Joseph Dudley Downing, born in 1925, near the very location of this family reunion, had returned home to be with a host of cousins, aunts, uncles, and other family members. In a sense, *all* of us had been born here; if you followed the winding highway from the cemetery, past the feed store and the only café in Fountain Run, to a crooked, bumpy dirt path that only a few of the Goodman elders could still find, you arrived at the very spot I mentioned earlier. My father took me there once at the end of a long afternoon of too many ham and biscuits and innings of baseball. The "home place" I had heard so much about was an overgrown, unmowed field; there were a few planks of weathered lumber lying on the ground near what might have been a stone foundation for a farmhouse. On that visit, I was antsy and ready to get back in the car. But I do remember a moment when I caught my father gazing through the imagined structure, beyond a rusty, falling-down barbed wire fence, and had the sense, just for a few seconds, that this place had meaning for him.

That was the reason Dudley had traveled thousands of miles to the family reunion. It was home.

As a journalist, I research and interview a number of people—both famous and not so famous. I realize, though, I should have been taking notes and talking with Dudley throughout his life, while he was still alive. The following observations have been constructed through documentary interviews, published material, and conversations with relatives who knew and visited him here and in France. He led a remarkable life.

He was one of eight children born to Aldridge Clifton and Katie Burton Goodman Downing. As a youngster, he had moved with his family about 20 miles from here to their tobacco farm in Horse Cave, Kentucky, located in Barren County.

The hilly terrain and the vast underground cave system below were a great influence on him as a painter. In an interview for a French documentary I saw, he described the vivid colors of the hills and valleys and the contrasting hue of the subterranean world beneath his feet as a "marvelous feast."

His older brother Dero, who became president of Western Kentucky University in Bowling Green, said, "At a very early age, Dud gave the signs and indications that he was unusually creative. In whatever surrounding he found himself, he had that unique capacity to find beauty in it."

"Above the ground," Dudley said in recorded comments, "it was the Kentucky hills and roses. It was so beautiful. And then underground, there was an enormous, impressive, awesome cave, with a river roaring through it. It was just fantastic."

At one time, the cave, which ran underneath the city of Horse Cave and was connected through a series of tunnels and passages to the vast Mammoth Cave system, was open to the public for tours. It was lit by electricity. By carefully making their way down a series of steps, tour guides pointed out the cave entrance as a half-sphere—the other half of the dome entrance having fallen away, giving growth to low-light vegetation. Dudley described his forays into the cave as a boy as high adventure.

"Deep in the cave, there are no lights. There was a darkness that can't be imagined—it is against your body, against your eyes. And when I was very young, I went down alone. I went back into the dark. I took my clothes off and got into the river. It was icy, icy cold, and everything was very black. You couldn't tell where the dark air stopped and the cold water started. It was very, very strange. Going back into the light from the dark—it was something that changed you up."

Dudley's work has been recognized for a unique combination of media and technique. He believed his personal artistic vision, which he proudly acknowledged was rooted in his Kentucky home place, has always been at the heart of his painting. He was once asked about the first time he picked up the brush. Did he paint as a child?

"No," Dudley replied shyly, "I made some paintings on black velvet for my mother. I was 18 maybe. It was something that leads to painting or being a painter. They were good."

But first, his life took a turn in another direction.

In 1943, he graduated as valedictorian of his high school class. Following his 18th birthday, in November of that year, he was inducted into the United States Army, where he served as an artillery observer in Europe during World War II. He was assigned to a unit that landed at Normandy soon after D-Day and the unit was engaged in a distinguished record of service until the end of the war. Dudley earned the Bronze Star with a citation for courage in action. While in Europe, he caught a brief glimpse of Paris, the city that would mean so much to his life and his career only a few years later. Dudley found the French countryside and its inhabitants as warm and inviting as his Kentucky home. He fell in love with the people.

His brother Dero said, "Dud loved people and made friends easily. He went with a family to milk their cows, if that was the timing of his visit at some rural home in France."

Dudley found the liberation of Paris the most romantic event of World War II. He later told his Kentucky friends of the supreme elation he felt during his short stint in The City of Light. He felt drawn to the same sights and sounds that had attracted American expatriates during the 1920s and 30s—F. Scott Fitzgerald, Gertrude Stein, Sherwood Anderson, and others. George Gershwin's musical production of *An American in Paris* and Josephine Baker's extravagant exploits on the stage made Paris an enchanting dream for many Americans. Before he attempted to officially take up the painter's brush, Dudley listened intently to stories of Maurice Chevalier's Paris, where love flourished and couples kissed on the metro and along the Seine late at night. He sauntered the Champs Elysees, the Place de la Concorde, and he might have sipped champagne in the bars at the Crillon and the Ritz Hotel where Hemingway made claims of personally liberating the most beautiful city in the world. During those heady days in Paris, when the late-afternoon light kissed the cathedral domes with a golden glow, Dudley vowed to return.

Following his return to the United States, he enrolled at Western Kentucky State Teachers College in Bowling Green for the 1945-46 school year. There, with encouragement from Professor Ivan Wilson, he began to recognize his enthusiasm for art. But, adhering to his parents' wishes and because an optometrist in Horse Cave was the only person with enough money to afford to drive a Cadillac, "where you could push buttons and the windows go up and down," Dudley said, he enrolled in the Northern Illinois College of Optometry in Chicago. Along with his optometry studies, he enrolled in night classes at the Chicago Art Institute and encountered the first great art he had ever been exposed to: European painters Degas and Picasso.

"I saw my first real painting when I went away to study optometry in Chicago at the age of 21. In a way, it was quite an advantage because I had never seen a good painting. I had never seen a bad painting. I had never seen many paintings at all," he mused.

"All of a sudden, the first paintings I saw were among the best paintings in the whole world—it was a revelation. It was like they had been waiting for me all of my life. It was marvelous, absolutely marvelous."

When he got to Chicago, he needed a place to stay. He discovered meat packer's row.

Dudley said, "All the very wealthy meat packers had put up palaces of one kind or another, so I went ringing door bells, asking if anyone had a room to rent. Finally, I rang a door bell, and this very lovely woman came to the door, long red hair that was all wet— she'd just washed her hair, and it was damp. She was rubbing her hair with a towel, and I told her of my mission and needed a place to stay."

She instructed Dudley to come back the following Tuesday night for dinner and promised a place for him in the house. Dudley was delighted and found that "she had united about 20 of the people I would have chosen out of the whole population of Chicago." Dudley said he was "set loose in a big beautiful city with all of its charm and dangers—both I welcomed with open arms. It was like being born again."

His associates at the house introduced him to books he had not read before. More important, his new friends took him to the Chicago Art Museum. Dudley had what he described as "a second awakening." When he discovered painting, he said, "I very quickly became a painter who was studying optometry or an optometry student who painted."

Dudley was a serious optometry student in Chicago, but his frequent trips to the Art Museum later defined his work as a painter. He credited the Post-Impressionists with first giving him ideas that he could put paint on the canvas. He relished his walks through the gallery and envied the style of the artists he observed: the vivid colors, thick application of paint, distinctive brush strokes, and large, oversized art. He studied their application of geometric form and real-life subject matter. He concentrated on the tiny dots of color that exemplified Georges Seurat, the swirling brush strokes Vincent van Gogh used to convey his feelings and state of mind, the stylistic categories of Fauvism and Cubism.

He reflected that his scientific studies in optometry had not been a distraction, but rather had enhanced his artistic side.

"I'm sure it is true of everybody in every field of endeavor, but for artists of all kinds there is nothing ever wasted. Everybody becomes a part of what you're doing. Optometry, in a very direct way, is a part of that. I had four years of study. Although it doesn't show in the paintings, it's very important to know how the ears are attached to the head— how the muscles are in the body—knowing this gives a foundation for doing anything," Dudley said.

He considered how his medical training had enhanced his painting. "We studied the psychology of color. We studied the physics of light, the anatomy of the eye, and what happens when vision occurs. All of this was very fine nourishment for artistic effort."

One of his Art Institute teachers taught him that "you can't teach painting, but you can teach a love of painting." In the city, Dudley often thought of his family. "My family had turned me loose in the hills of Kentucky, and now I was turned loose in the museum—barefoot in both places—if not physically, at least morally barefoot."

For Dudley, these were carefree but reckless days. His intense medical study routine and his love of painting began to clash when he began to drink too much near the conclusion of his optometry classes, falling in with a group of young writers and painters whose nightlong talk of art and life intoxicated him.

In 1950, he graduated from optometry school and decided to take some time off before settling into a medical practice somewhere. By chance, he received a war-insurance refund from the federal government totaling $300. Using that, he scraped together enough to get to Paris. Except for an occasional trip home, he lived in France the rest of his life.

His brother Dero remembers: "He got over there and walked the banks of the Seine and visited great art places and became further infatuated with France. He wrote me and asked me to explain to our parents he was going to remain there."

Dear Dee,

I trust this letter finds you and yours doing well. I am discovering daily the beauty and enchantment that is Paris. The sense of peace and serenity I am finding in this place has forced a realization; this is where I want to be. It is my ambition to be a successful painter. The thing I will miss most is the nearness and opportunity to be with family. But I won't let it separate us. After all—shouldn't all children have one uncle who disappears for 20 years and returns with a beard and scarf that no one knows where he got them? If you could, explain to Mom and Dad this is where I intend to remain and I hope they will understand. And if you will do that for me, I'll appreciate it.

Much love, Dud

Part II:
Paris, Painting, and Picasso

"I love Paris in the spring time
I love Paris in the fall
I love Paris in the winter when it drizzles
I love Paris in the summer when it sizzles"
-Cole Porter

Joseph Dudley Downing, native of Horse Cave, Kentucky, graduate of the Northern Illinois College of Optometry School in Chicago, Illinois, found Paris exciting and exhilarating. He often said, "This is where I was meant to be." Dudley took a three-month excursion to Paris in 1950 and stayed for 58 years. Dud's letter to his brother articulating his desire to remain in France was delivered to his parents. Dero said, "As loving parents, they wanted him to be happy. They understood the major currents of life sufficiently and, having reared seven children who were the beneficiaries of parents who were devoted, loving, caring, supportive—that's the manner in which they accepted his decision to do that in 1950."

What did young Dudley first encounter in the City of Light? Where did his exploration in the cultural capital of the Western world take him? Might he have walked to the corner where the Rue Saint-Jacques met the Rue Soufflot and gazed across the Seine toward the 15th century Tour Saint-Jacques rising out of the mists of the river? He felt swept into the very depths of the city's intellect, sensuality, and historical legacy.

I believe Dudley had packed his Kentucky belongings in a crumpled, cracked leather suitcase—the kind that has twin straps encircling the gear, buckling in front—and along with his razor and shirts had stowed away a tattered copy of Hemingway's *The Sun Also Rises*, whose stripped, spare prose changed the way everyone after him wrote the English language. Dudley became part of the cast of 30-something dissolute expatriates—maybe the sardonic novelist

Bill Gorton or the narrator Jack Barnes—who frequented the cafés near the intersection of the Boulevard Montparnasse and the Boulevard Raspail, where Hemingway went often to write.

Dudley said, "There, my Lord, I burst into flower one more time. A wilted flower probably, not a hesitant flower, but I flowered one more time because being there, looking up the river and down the river, I thought this is for me, this is wonderful. I feel right," he declared. "This feels like I'm at home here."

Initially, he was like any typical tourist, whipping through all of the familiar sights at top speed—Notre Dame, the Sainte-Chapelle, Napoleon's Tomb, and the Louvre, where fate and considerable talent brought him years later. Braving his vertigo, he ascended the Eiffel Tower, soaring above the city's southern skyline to marvel at the amazing iron construction and the striking views it offered from any perspective. He realized he could not properly savor the city unless he curbed his frenetic pace and became an aimless stroller in a city invented for aimless strolling.

On a typical early December day—the cold and damp blanketing the streets, the buildings, the sky—Dudley would zigzag through ancient cobblestone streets to meet with students at the Sorbonne. He would pause at a small round table with solid-wood cane chairs, extract a few francs from the pocket of his wool sweater, and order a croissant or brioche and a café creme, the Paris-brewed coffee served in the morning. Later in the day, for only about 400 francs (about one U.S. dollar), he would load his lunch tray with a small piece of rabbit in cream-and-mustard sauce, a salad, a wedge of cheese, bread, and a carafe of red wine. The goal was, of course, to be part of the scene, to read the *Paris Tribune* with one eye on the paper, one eye scanning the ever-changing human landscape.

And if, by chance, or on purpose, while near the Sorbonne and the College de France, amid the bustle of students and intellectuals, he found his way to the cafes along the Boulevard St. Germain and a sighting of the dean of existentialism, Jean-Paul Sartre, sipping a coffee with friends and scholarly associates? Ah, Dudley was truly at the corner of today and tomorrow.

Dressed in rough wool pants, turtleneck, and a sports jacket purchased from a second-hand store—a package of French filterless cigarettes stashed in the coat pocket—Dudley saw more art, sculptures, public monuments, paintings, than he could have imagined. Sauntering along the Seine among the pigeons pecking for the crumbs, he recalled the only two reproductions he had gazed upon as a grade-school student in Kentucky. On the walls of the elementary school classroom was the 1851 oil-on-canvas painting by the German American artist Emanuel Gottlieb Leutze of *Washington Crossing the Delaware* and Georges Seurat's *A Sunday on La Grande.* The latter painting came to life for Dudley when he visited the "big platter," an island in the River Seine, where he saw a potpourri of people strolling, lounging, rowing, and fishing in the park. He was influenced by Seurat's pointillism technique of rendering his subjects by placing tiny precise brush strokes of different colors close to one another so that they blended at a distance. Did he see the exacting contours, geometric shapes, and measured proportions in his own work?

If the Parisian writing community congregated on the Left Bank, generations of painters hung out at the top of the Right Bank, in Montmartre. Dudley's research led him to the Impressionists, Monet and Cezanne, and the post-Impressionists Toulouse-Lautrec, Georges Braque, and others. Picasso developed Cubism, a profound revolution in modern art, while living here, another watermark for a young American painter in France struggling with his own style and expression.

From the 1950s to the early 1960s, Paris gallery owners estimated there were about 100 serious American painters working in Paris. Dudley began with a routine familiar to so many painters: working at a day job, making art in the evening. He described a dreary little hotel on the Rue Dauphine "where you cooked under a sign that said 'cooking prohibited.'" He took scraps of specially treated paper and fastened them together with a stapler. He scoured the streets and shops for other materials, finding value in preserving what others had tossed aside. He denuded bits of old wills, marriage licenses, and birth certificates—the documents of life itself.

"I found an old registry for the days of absence of the employees of city hall in Paris from 1912 to 1932. And the writing was very beautiful—little, tiny, meticulous hand writing, the same writing through those same years. I picked it up because the paper was very, very, very beautiful handmade paper, and I took it home for the paper. Then I saw these years covered the First World War and the days of absence of those men were very poignant and that they almost, to a man, had been mobilized for the war. I got interested when they came back—they came back on compassionate or sick leave—most of them returned safely."

In his small room, dimly lit by a swinging light bulb, Dudley, clothed in a painter's smock and bright, red-checkered bandana, hovered over the registry and began to paint on, around, and beside the names he found fascinating. "It wasn't on purpose. I felt we knew each other well enough, and I wanted to paint on that paper. It happens like that. I don't really choose it." His "paintings" brought French art critics under his spell.

He applied the same artistry and style to an old, discarded window frame he found on one of his missions to collect materials. "The window, I like it when they're old. The window is 300 years old. After 300 years, the people who had been living behind it for 75 years decided that maybe it had served them long enough, and they wanted a new window," he remarked with a smile. "As they were taking it down, I asked for it. I was looking at what to do in the framework, and I remembered the early Dutch painters painted on red copper and so it is red copper where the glass used to be. Those things happen instead of being searched for."

Engrossed in the Paris art scene, the novice artist got a break with his first exhibition in 1952. The show not only brought attention to his work, it also brought an encounter with a kindly bald-headed man who dropped by and stayed for about 20 minutes. That gentleman was the master, Pablo Picasso. Dudley recalled the afternoon well and said with fondness, "The gallery had a big glass window in front, and I was reading in the back and working on some lan pshades when a shadow fell on the floor. I looked up, and Picasso was peering in the window. And I will never know if his interest was in the lampshades that I had worked on or the painting. I was very careful to keep my gaze down until I heard his footsteps come into the center of the room, and I looked up and there he stood. There was an extraordinary feeling, of course. I turned pink, I turned red. I almost jumped up and down on the spot, but was careful to be discreet," Dudley reminisced. "He looked around, and then he came to speak to me. He told me he liked the exhibition. 'Well done,' he commented. With wrinkled fingers, Picasso searched his pants pocket for a business card and instructed Dudley that when his work had changed sufficiently, to bring some things to show him. Charmed and delighted by their chance rendezvous, Dudley waited two years before he saw Picasso again. "I brought small pieces for him to see, and he gave me encouragement and hope. He said, 'Work hard, be true to yourself.' It was a marvelous experience. He was very kind."

Although still working at a law office each afternoon as a sort of office boy, Dudley's reputation as an artist mounted steadily. Critics began to review and characterize his growing body of work. He was never an action painter, they wrote, but spontaneous and impetuous. He "painted" with a razor and palette knife, turning out rough-textured canvases. Some were composed of great oblong globs of glowing color, others matted threads that circled and swooped, but never tangled.

Hunkered over his work bench, long-bladed, sturdy shears in hand, he snipped away with short, quick strokes, experimenting with different media—leather, canvas, fabric, wood, and bone. "I still considered easel painting, oil painting on canvas the most interesting for me, and my most important engagement. But, very quickly, paintings as intricate as mine have decided to be—and very quickly the doors close on a day's work. Suddenly, I've learned, you must leave a painting to rest a little—to see your way through." It was during these periods that Dudley used scissors. "If I'm going to make a composition on one of my columns, I use little cobbler's tacks for nailing. They're very handsome, and no two heads are exactly alike. They're not quite rounding, and they're sharper than tacks. Turns out they're perfect for my use with painted leather on wood."

These columns or panels are tall and narrow—sometimes only a foot or two in width and can stand eight to 10 feet high. The stapleages had nutty titles: "Once is Not a Custom," "Miss Brown to You," "Panic in Harem." In 1961, within a few days of an exhibition opening at the Galerie Arnaud, more than half of the compositions were sold. Dudley learned that "the fact of cutting canvas or leather and nailing it to wood will only loosen me up to get back to easel painting."

With a growing notoriety and spotlight on his work, but no consistent income, Dudley found touring the French countryside a relaxing and inexpensive way to recharge his energies for more painting. On a serendipitous trip to the heart of Provence, Dudley and his companions stopped in Menerbes, one of France's "perched villages." The town is spread out on top of a hill that rises from a variety of agricultural fields, vineyards, and cherry orchards. He knew that Picasso had lived in this little village known not for its painters, but its truffles, wine, cheese, and opulent Christmas market. Like any little town balanced on the high rocks, Menerbes offered numerous viewpoints: one view of the mountain Luberon, another of the farm valley below and the red-roof tiles of the dwellings built up and into the mountain. Dudley found it peaceful and noticed right away that during certain times of the day, the sunlight, which streamed through the streets, around corners and into open windows, would be superb for painting.

"We came to Menerbes by chance, my friend Manuel and me, and had the habit of spending 15 days with an old friend. We swam every year and profited from the sea. Neither of us knew how to drive. Our friend said 'I'm tired of lugging you two boys around. There's a very beautiful little town here and we'll stop and spend the night.'" In a documentary about him, Joe's face brightens and breaks into a warm grin when he talks about Menerbes. "The next morning, I got up earlier than the other people and went out for a little walk in the village and followed a very pretty little bird dog up the hill. The dog, long-legged and skinny, long ears, led me past a tumbled-down-looking place where I found sitting in the front of his house a farmer. He had written on the top of a shoebox with a piece of chalk 'Ruins for Sale.' So I stopped to talk to him, and he took me to see the ruins. Immediately, I knew I wanted them very much—they were the only things I could see in the sun that I could afford. The heart of it for me was the studio." The ruins eventually became his house and studio for the rest of his life.

Dudley's love for the house and studio were romanticized in an ode to his country place:

Two walls with windows,
One wall without.
At the rear, the village backbone, raw rock.
My easel stands erect, ladder or gallows.
Outside, a roof,
Its rounded tiles freckled and tan
Attentive to the sun like dinosaur eggs,
Spotted gray and yellow with lichen.
Outside also life clings to the wall,
A climbing rose,
Passion flower,
Wisteria, flaming bush.
Together and each in turn they flower,
Move,
Give off their perfume,
Absorb or reflect light of the sun, light of the moon,
Are rinsed by rain, by dew.
Far off, the rocks and trees of the Luberon chain
And its undulant line barring the sky.
Sky, mountain, stub-limbed locust tree,
Little wild garden, window, easel, brush.
There is the most silent of noises.
Bristles on linen.
In the heat, grass grows,
Its seed fall.
A dog barks.

The house transformed Dudley and became another ingredient in his life of color and light that continued the rebirth he felt so deeply when he first decided to leave America for Paris. Escaping the city during the warmer months of the year, Dudley used Menerbes as an oasis for his mind and growing body of work.

The house was part of a very large complex of rooms and rock with the back wall of the studio made up of part of the village's limestone cliff. "It influences what I think and what I do. The front gives out onto a very beautiful, very, very old tile roof. There is a very wonderful old, old, old locust tree; no one knows how old it is." Dudley said, "And then back of that there is the mountain and the hills. So, this too, is conducive to painting."

Vines and brush covered the stone walls that surrounded the house. In the summer, windows and doors opened to the wind that invited itself in with the cats and dogs that roamed freely through the house and the small garden, lush with emerald moss and vines.

"I think the most important work is done in the morning. I'm up around seven o'clock. I'm the cook in our little establishment, so by 7:30, I'm down walking Daisy the dog and going shopping. I like very much going shopping for food, and usually by the time I make breakfast, everybody is sort of settling in. It's 10, and I go to the studio. I work from 10 until one and make lunch. It doesn't require too much effort—a little rest after that and I'm back in the studio from three to five—the schedule is very elastic. It depends on what I want to do and what I feel like doing, but it's every day and has become so ingrained as a part of my life over the years that I don't even think about it anymore."

"It's the central part of my life, and it's where I come every day—short periods sometimes long. It's where the painting grows. They grow up in families—like families they have strong bonds with each other, but each takes on a life very early. Every day I'm surprised to be physically and geographically where I am."

Dudley felt comfortable in Menerbes. Summering in the south of France opened his eyes and his sensibilities to the region and all it offered. The physical presence of being in Menerbes—moving about the village shops, talking with residents, strolling the narrow walkways—rekindled the fire that transferred to the canvas. Escaping Paris each year was invigorating, and, if he had ever lost touch with his Kentucky roots, southern France heightened his allegiance to his birthplace.

"The big change in my palette was the physical and geographical change from painting in Paris to painting in the south—painting in Provence—my palette exploded. The bright colors came because I was living in bright colors. I spend half the time in this little town that is exactly the same size as Horse Cave. It is constituted of farmers and people who serve farmers, and I felt very much at home. In Paris, I lead practically the same life I led in Horse Cave—seeing a few friends, cooking, eating, and painting a little."

Kentucky had left such an indelible mark on Dudley's life,

and in Menerbes he found some of what had shaped him. Remembering Kentucky, Dudley described warm, endless summer days when children were "turned loose" to roam the hillsides and bicycle the uncluttered streets of Horse Cave, stopping in at the drugstore for a soft drink and snack. Then, it was off to the woods where small minds were occupied with the Indians who lived there before. "Life was full of discoveries," and for Dudley, Horse Cave and Menerbes both had the same sort of promise.

Dudley recalled how the smallest things in his youth shaped the very brushstrokes he applied to the canvas.

"On a visit back home, I was sleeping at my sister's farm and one morning, very early, in the summer, she called me. It was about six in the morning. She said, 'Come, come look, there is something very beautiful.' So I went, and it was a spider's web that was just being finished by the spider. But I knew she had not called me just for that—we'd seen that thousands of times. She said, 'Wait and watch.' The web had little drops of dew, and they were catching the light. And the spider, when it had finished the web, the architecture part, went back to the beginning on the left, and started weaving again."

Dudley raised his gnarled fingers to form a minute opening between his thumb and forefinger and continued to describe what he had seen. "In the bands were tiny, tiny little symbols, little letters with figures, and my sister said this is the secretary spider—what she weaves is the date of the end of the world, but up until now no one has been able to read it. And, so when I saw the bands not quite distinguishable—there are some figures showing in my paintings—I knew I had to thank my sister Elizabeth and the spider."

Dudley used these little symbols—colorful triangles, squares, round circles saturated with hues of dark and light tints—on a growing variety of surfaces, from canvas to indurate exteriors. He said, "Something cries out to be painted on." He wandered the streets of Paris and the countryside of Menerbes to discover whatever might draw his brush to its surface.

"The roof tiles I painted on come from this house—my house was much bigger when I got it—and, in 300 years, there were more roof tiles than roof. I've been painting on them for some time now—their very surface is appealing. It takes paint well; it's like a very good paper. They are nice to touch and see. It wasn't as though I looked for roof tiles. It was the same sense I had about the register paper. Something calls out to me to be painted on."

Although Dudley's work is owned by prestigious museums and collectors around the world—he holds the distinction of being one of three Americans to exhibit work at the Louvre (the other two are James Abbott McNeill Whistler and Mark Tobey)—Dudley was always interested in bringing his work home to Kentucky. An arboretum and museum was constructed in Bowling Green on the property of a benefactor, Jerry Baker. Dudley's largest collection is housed there, including two massive barn doors from a hillside farm in Provence.

"Someone told me about a big pair of barn doors on a farm not far from Menerbes that were being sold by the owner. He was a healer—he lay on hands. I called them 'Isadore's Doors'—someone named Isadore had carved his name into them and they sat at my house for 11 years before I touched them to paint them because they were so handsome in themselves they defied any embellishment, and I was very proud the doors were finding a new life."

Stooped by age, shuffling from a dining-room table to the chair sitting in front of his easel, his fingers crippled and bent with arthritis, Dudley squeezed a paint tube, wiping the edges on the side of the palette. He grasped the brush, dabbed the end with paint, and gently kissed the canvas with an azure tint like that of a clear and unclouded sky. His outlook on life, his daily routine of painting every day, and the optimism he inherited from his mother highlighted and guided the brush.

"My mother was pathologically optimistic. Optimism beyond reason. When I was six years old, my mother sent me to the cellar to get potatoes, and she gave me a basket and she said bring back the biggest potato every day, the biggest potato. Even when the biggest one is smallest, no bigger than a marble—believe it is the biggest, believe it is the best."

This eternal gift carried Dudley throughout the remaining years of his life in France.

Joe Downing with two large framed stapleages (staple collages) in front of the Facchetti Gallery, at the time of his first "real" gallery exhibition

Joe in the early 1950s

Joe Downing with Emmanuel Wardi in their studio apartment in Paris

Joe Downing talking with Thérèse Paret and Emmanuel Wardi in the Maid's Room, Rue de l'université

Joe in Paris apartment

Joe getting ready to hang his first exhibition with the Facchetti Gallery in 1953, Rue de Lille, Paris

Joe in his studio in Paris (Photograph by Brigitte Meuwissen)

Joe in his garden in Menerbes (Photograph by André Morain)

Joe in his studio in Menerbes

Untitled, oil on canvas by Joe Downing (Photograph by Emily Hendricksen)

Of Men and the Mountain: Conquering Rainier

As the rented SUV rounded the corner of the highway from Seattle, I saw the mountain for the first time.

For miles, we had been surrounded by small groves of aspen and towering fir trees. The day was cool and overcast, with just enough cloud cover to keep the peak of Mount Rainier hidden. It was now midmorning, the sun coming out. Craning my neck up and toward the top of the car window, I could just barely see what I thought might be the summit of the most prominent mountain in the contiguous United States. I was stunned by what I saw.

It wasn't just the height. It was the mass of the entire body of the promontory that grabbed my attention. There was something about seeing it from that particular angle—the sloping meadow dotted with snow, boulders that looked like pebbles in the shadow of the mountain, the sheer scope and scale of the broad expanse of what appeared to be the base of the rock.

It took my breath away.

In the packed vehicle, piled high with boots and backpacks, this noisy group of climbing partners fell silent, all of us trying to understand just what we were seeing.

It was August 1993. The beginning of our adventure had started serendipitously. A group of us, 15 or so in number, ranging in age from early 20s to early 50s, had begun planning a trip to Mount Rainier National Park. As residents of Glasgow, Kentucky, we were all experienced hikers, familiar with the Appalachian Trail in the fall, winter, and spring months. There had been "adventure vacations" to Glacier National Park in Montana and the Wind River Range in Wyoming, and extensive hiking excursions over mountainous terrain in Colorado in the summer.

We thought we knew what to expect on Rainier.

As flatlanders from Kentucky, void of any mountain-climbing experience whatsoever, but emboldened by the spirit and camaraderie that overtakes wise judgment and replaces it with the insanity of a moment, our minds had told us that this adventure was in the bag. After all, John Muir had climbed Rainier in 1888, before Gore-Tex, rain suits, and crampons. It has been reported that he enjoyed the view, but conceded that it was best appreciated from below. How tough could reaching the summit of Rainier be?

To prepare for the trip, I had read extensively about the mountain and its topography, the fitness and equipment required to scale it, and the possibility of death. About three mountaineering deaths occur each year on Rainier due to rock and ice fall, avalanches, and the falls and hypothermia associated with severe weather. The worst accident on Rainier occurred in 1981, when 11 people lost their lives in an ice fall on one of the glaciers. In the summer of 2010, four climbing deaths were reported on Rainier. In 2012, a park ranger died while attempting a rescue.

In my reading, I became fascinated by the effect of high altitudes on the human body. In its most dangerous form, altitude sickness can progress to pulmonary edema and cerebral edema—two ailments no one wanted. I found it interesting that the causes of altitude sickness are not fully understood. It commonly occurs above 8000 feet, presenting a collection of nonspecific symptoms resembling the flu, carbon monoxide poisoning, or a hangover, and is often accompanied by a bad headache. It is difficult to determine ahead of time who will be affected by altitude sickness. Most people can climb to 8000 feet without problems. But you never know. After years of research, scientists do know this: ascending slowly is the best way to avoid becoming ill. Most experts tell you "to stop and go" up the mountain, walking in short bursts.

One suggestion that experienced climbers and guides always pass along to people climbing at high altitude for the first time is to acclimate. That's the process of adjusting to less oxygen at higher elevations by spending a few hours or a day at a higher altitude, then descending, then going back to that altitude or higher, then descending to help your body adjust to the elevation.

Of course, that's all well and good if you live near a mountain. But if you're on a week's vacation and don't have the time to go through this process, you have to wait until you're at the higher elevation to practice. A couple of other medical tips seem to help, including medication, but that comes later in this story.

I was here because I had been adopted by the hikers and their wives. Most of the group had been together for years, hiking, camping, rafting (and sometimes imbibing to excess) in the wilderness. They were a jolly group and fun to be around. Arriving back in Glasgow, my boyhood home, after years spent out of state, I found them gracious and accommodating. I had been in the Boy Scouts with many of them as a youngster, but had a lot of catching up to do and camping equipment to purchase before I could be considered one of them.

My first hiking expedition with the group had been a disaster thanks to a tiny, bright-orange, Kmart-type pup tent that leaked at the seams, stiff hiking boots that weren't waterproof, a meal plan that needed more thought and flavor, and gear that weighed way too much. Our leader Louie (aka the trailmeister) had chosen Walnut Bottoms, an area nestled in the Great Smoky Mountain National Park near Gatlinburg, for our expedition. It rained close to 10 inches the first night, and everything I had remained soaked for the rest of the trip. On the second day, we hiked in a downpour to a lookout fire tower. At the top of the knoll, where the fire tower overlooked thousands of acres of parkland, one of the more experienced hikers tried in vain to start a fire to warm our wet clothes and chilling bodies. The wood shavings, leaves, and bits of paper were not enough to create one.

After hours of slogging through the woods, we called it a day, returning to camp in the late afternoon only to discover that two of our party had abandoned the tent site and left for parts unknown. To this day, my cousin Joe swears they relocated to higher and drier ground. The rest of us think they went to the Holiday Inn.

My first backpacking adventure with the boys since returning to Kentucky ended on Sunday, but subsequent trips, better equipment and tastier food led me to the base of one of the largest mountains in the world. Several from this contingent of hikers also signed up for the Rainier adventure.

We were a curious lot. Louie, a pulmonologist, planned out all of our hiking trips. Part daredevil, part hero, he was always the first one in the water, never knowing the exact depth or if a big limb might be just below the surface. It was, of course, his idea to climb

Mount Rainier. He'd be the first one on the mountain.

Benny, Louie's cousin and a district-court judge, was the intellectual among us. Maybe not the most athletic or in shape, but always with a historical biography under his arm and a quick retort to anyone who said he wasn't ready to attack the mountain.

There was Phil, a lawyer, and his wife, Margie, well-traveled and experienced hikers; Butch, a cardiologist, cerebral and analytical. We all felt a bit more comfortable with Dr. Butch on the trip. Sam, Benny's son and a financial adviser, was the youngest and proved it with his bravado and tales of conquest, outdoors and otherwise. Cousin Joe, the one we believed to have gone to the Holiday Inn near Gatlinburg, had elected not to climb the mountain, but instead headed up the support team back at the national park lodge bar.

Why did we decide to climb Mount Rainier? Why not one of the Colorado "Fourteeners" first? Why not attempt Mount Elbert, the tallest peak in Colorado, which has been described as a tough, but a nontechnical hike to the top? Why not take the Mount Whitney Trail to the top, which, at 14,505 feet, is the highest summit in the contiguous United States? Rainier is a more visible mountain, its summit exposed for all to see on clear days. During winter months, a light mist can hide the snow-white top for weeks. Mount Whitney is hidden by neighboring slopes and rock outcroppings and only comes into view occasionally as you make your way up to the peak. So I guess you could say the reason why perhaps is we honed in on the majesty of Mount Rainier.

George Leigh Mallory is probably not on anybody's list of familiar names. But three words he uttered probably are familiar to most. When asked by a *New York Times* reporter in 1923 why he wanted to climb Mount Everest, the British mountaineer said, "Because it's there." Mallory and a companion died a year later on the slopes of Everest. I'm not sure the group preparing to tackle Rainier ever had a serious discussion about why we were attempting this challenging mountain or what the possible consequences might be if one of us had a problem on the side of this snowy, icy, windy, crevasse-laden and, yes, dangerous pile of rocks. We had talked about the proper equipment, the danger of "snow blindness," and how many vehicles we were going to lease for the week— but we had never talked about the "what if" factor.

Sir Edmund Hillary, one of the most famous mountain climbers in the world and the first man to successfully climb Nepal's Mount Everest, once said, "It is not the mountain we conquer, but ourselves." Each one of us had a reason. And that was good enough. On clear days Mount Rainier dominates the southeastern horizon of the Northwest. It is the most heavily glaciated peak in the lower 48. People who live in Washington State and Canada say that on clear days, the mountain can be seen as far away as Portland, Oregon, and Victoria, British Columbia. It is still an active volcano. Climbing on Mount Rainier is difficult, involving traversing the largest glaciers in the United States south of Alaska.

According to records available at Mount Rainier, some 8000 to 13000 people attempt the climb each year; about 90 percent use the Camp Muir route. This is the path we took. In most of the United States, a hike of 3000 vertical feet to the summit of a peak is considered about average; 4000 to 5000 feet is considered a very long and tiring trip; and anything above 6000 is rare and difficult.

Mount Rainier, by its easiest route, requires ascending 9000 vertical feet.

Rainier Mountaineering Incorporated has been guiding climbs on the mountain and all over the world for over 40 years. RMI was founded by Lou Whitaker, a Seattle native who has distinguished himself not only as a guide and mountaineer, but as a businessman and lecturer. He is legendary, an iconic figure to whom I spoke early one morning in the hotel dining room.

The stated goals of RMI, according to their website, are to assist clients in attaining the summit, encouraging respect and understanding of the alpine environment, as well as educating through the adventures of mountaineering and offering the most enjoyable and rewarding alpine experience possible.

I've been around sports and athletes all my life, but I've never seen a more fit group of men and women, at the top of the strength and endurance scale, than the guides I met and observed on Mount Rainier. RMI guides have only a few hours to instruct the hundreds who come through their mountaineering school each day in preparation for a summit hike. And many of the neophytes in our Kentucky climbing group would need help in all facets of the skills required to be safe and summit, from the simplest technique of efficient mountain travel, like rest-stepping and pressure breathing, to the more coordinated use of crampons and ice axes. We would be in the first grade all over again.

All of us, some more than others, had been previously schooled in the more obvious details of climbing. We knew that the more time spent getting in shape, the better. The plan was to be in the best shape of our lives. Cardiovascular training like running, biking, hiking, strength training and weight work was necessary prep. On summit day, we would be on our feet from early morning until late afternoon with only a few rest breaks for water and food. The task seemed more and more daunting after hearing the guides explain what to expect in a little over 24 hours.

After a nice evening at the hotel in Paradise at the national park, we were all ready the next morning for RMI's mountaineering day school. The guides taught us equipment orientation, and hiking and climbing techniques. Inside an old building a short distance from the hotel, the guides led us through a tutorial on how our helmets should fit, what carabineers to hang on our pack, and where and how a load of 60 pounds should feel on shoulders and hips. The guides were matter-of-fact in their instruction, courteous and helpful, but all business. We had been told in advance what gear to bring and what we needed to rent at the RMI headquarters. Besides needing standard hiking gear, including a good backpack, with either an internal or external frame that fit comfortably, clothing mattered, we were told. We had to layer for both warm weather walking and the below-freezing temperatures we would encounter on the mountain. We practiced how to use an ice axe: a multi-purpose metal tool that has a very sharp point at the end of the handle called a spike, and two serrated blade-like devices at the other end. Climbers use the tool as a walking stick when traveling uphill. The pointed pick and head element can be buried in the ice and snow if a person begins falling. It is a forbidding, lethal instrument that looks like it could be used by a serial killer.

Another piece of equipment are crampons—razor-sharp attachments that fit on boots, necessary for providing traction on ice and snow. Made of steel or aluminum, crampons either clip on or are fitted to the boot through an elaborate leather strap system that taxes even the most dexterous when applying them in the middle of the night with freezing temperatures that chill fingertips. They are cumbersome and make stepping up or down the mountain difficult. It is easy to accidentally hang the sharp, pointed end of the crampon spike in a cuff or stray boot strap, which can cause you to topple over. But it is almost impossible to traverse the mountain slope without them.

And then there were the various and sundry other pieces of gear and clothing that our guide suggested: plastic boots; gloves; a cap, helmet and proper sunglasses to prevent snow blindness; a climbing harness; rope. The list and the expenses went on. It was a far cry from donning a pair of running shoes and shorts and leaving the house for a jog.

RMI's mountaineering school and one-day training is recognized worldwide for its professionalism. These athletes also practice a little psychology with a physical and mental assessment of each person signed up for the trip. After departing headquarters at the base camp, the guides, five to seven of them, accompany about 20 people to the training area. They hike beside you, talk to you about your experience as a hiker or climber, observe your breathing pattern in the higher altitude, and assess whether or not you could keep up the pace. They make a determination that first morning whether you have "the right stuff" to make it. Later, on the trip itself, that becomes important, if not a little unnerving.

Training started on a beautiful, clear, sun-splashed morning. The guides established a brisk pace that had already left a few people behind on the same well-worn path we would follow the next day to begin our summit assault. It was exhilarating to finally be on the mountain doing what we had dreamed of doing for months.

Carrying only a light pack, but juggling with the ice axe, crampons, rope, and other items, I tried to look the part of the experienced alpinist going for a routine hike up a mountain. But to no avail. I felt anxious about what might lie ahead.

There was little conversation. Everyone concentrated on the quick pace set by the lead guide.

"How's everyone doing?" asked Elizabeth, as we trudged toward the practice area. After an hour or so, with Rainier looming far above us, our boots crunched snow for the first time. The guides had chosen a slope with a small incline of perhaps 200 yards from top to bottom with about a 45 degree grade on which we would practice the basics of mountaineering.

With patience, the guides watched us. When we needed it, they provided instruction in the rudiments of attaching crampons, lacing and weaving the long strands of leather strapping in and out of the eyelets to be sure the crampon stayed fastened to the boot; and the proper carrying technique of the ice axe, handle reversed, sharp spike facing backward, handle strap on your wrist.

Use of the ice axe was conducted with precision. At the top of the slope, we practiced self-arrest, a procedure that teaches you to jam the head of the ice axe into the snow in the event you begin to topple down the hill. We also practiced "falling," both the movement itself and the yelling of the word at the top of our lungs, an alert to the climbing party, should someone lose footing or balance. Falling can occur when on your own or roped to a team.

Here's how we practiced it: First, on our backs, or faces down, heads toward the bottom of the hill, the guides held our feet to keep us from sliding, then let go so that we sailed down toward the bottom. We had to plunge the pick into the snow, stopping our momentum so we didn't careen into a deep crevasse.

Instruction went quickly. The guides included a strapping, Russian-born mountain of a man with a thick accent; Elizabeth, blonde with bright blue eyes, who had put her San Francisco law career on hold to guide neophytes up and down mountain slopes; and Chip, the all-American guy who was all fun and games the day of the training, but turned serious and steady on our excursion.

And then there was Sirjai—a small-framed, quiet Nepali Sherpa who had been recruited as an authentic, veteran mountain climber and guide. Who better to receive instruction from than a native of the Mount Everest region who had climbed on many of the world's tallest peaks? Sirjai had taught the other guides the walking technique known as the "rest-step," a halting, walking gait used when ascending steep slopes. It takes practice, but its most important characteristic is a pause of motion with the rear leg vertical and extended, knee locked, while the front leg is relaxed. It is used to rest the weight of your body on your lower limbs. He also demonstrated "pressure-breathing": exhaling air in quick, short bursts to facilitate oxygen-carbon dioxide exchange at high altitudes. It is also known as the "Whitaker Wheeze" because of the sound made when blowing out the air through the mouth.

Then it was down the mountain, a few beers, a nice dinner, and packing for the first leg of the journey the next day. At dinner, we were excited about what the next two days might bring. We didn't all share the same comfort or confidence level. I could tell there were two or three in our group who were beginning to doubt whether they could make it.

The next morning we were once again blessed with a clear, sparkling day. The group, about 25 hopefuls, gathered at the Paradise base camp, divided up into rope teams of six to eight per length of rope, and started up Mount Rainier.

The guides were cheerful, encouraging, and kept up a quick pace up the trail. Our day hike took us to Camp Muir, where we overnighted. The trail up the Muir snowfield begins at 5400 feet; Muir is at 10,000, so we had quite a steep but invigorating morning walk. By mid-morning, the weather had warmed, and we were in shorts and t-shirts. In a couple of hours, our long string of hikers found itself even with or slightly above low-level clouds.

During a short pause to rest, balancing on a trekking pole, I glanced backward several thousand feet to the lodge and national park buildings below. By then, they were tiny, toy-like objects. Other climbers were making their way toward us. The mountain was full of life, alive with bustling bodies. I wondered why everyone was in such a hurry.

For a moment, I thought of all the climbers who had come before me to tackle this pile of rocks. For each of us, the reason was different. Some simple, some complex. Was it just a feat, another notch on the belt of physical accomplishments that included triathlons and 100-mile cycling events? Or, was it something deeper, a conquest for the mind rather than the body? Each of us had a reason to be on Mount Rainier that day. For me, it was partly physical, but primarily the tremendous mental challenge.

Soon, the small, square buildings of Camp Muir appeared at the base of a rocky ridge called Cowlitz Cleaver. The trip from Paradise is a five-hour hike. As the sun began to drop, the dry mountain air began to warn of the colder temperatures that were only hours away. Around four o'clock, someone from the rear shouted out, "There it is!" and the black, wooden box of the Camp Muir bunkhouse appeared. There was a quick scramble to secure a sleeping area for the short night. Climbers aren't promised plush accommodations—we were packed into the bunkhouse like sardines. The structure is small and crammed with a few bunks and an open sleeping area where you could crawl into your bag. There may have been room just inside the only entrance for a couple of gas stoves when the weather prohibited cooking outside. Many of the climbers who had been here before brought tents and slept outdoors where it was less crowded.

We ate freeze-dried food and Clif bars for dinner before watching a sunset at 10,000 feet, the perfect way to conclude our trip to Camp Muir. At that altitude, the setting sun was a sight I had only seen from an airplane or in pictures and films; the rays burned through layers of fluffy clouds below us as we perched on a rock tabletop outside the bunkhouse.

None of us could help feeling nervous about the next day. Our group huddled together as the temperature began to fall toward the freezing mark, quietly speaking to one another about our individual readiness and openly admitting some trepidation. All agreed to at least start out together. We hoped to reach the summit and return to Paradise safely in 24 hours.

We were in our bunks at six o'clock, but I slept very little. Too many people, too much noise, uncomfortable conditions. Knowing what I faced the next day, I'm not sure a five-star hotel and a sleeping pill would have helped.

Everyone was roused out of their bags at midnight. This early wake up is called an alpine start. We wanted to get up the mountain and on the summit before the heat of day brought in inclement weather. The guides heated enough water for a quick bowl of oatmeal. While forcing the midnight snack down, we rearranged equipment, strapped on crampons, donned awkward fitting helmets, affixed axes to backpacks, and joined our rope teams. We would remain roped together until our return to Muir.

By one o'clock, we were on our way. It was a cool, clear night. A surreal feeling surrounded me as I began the task of stumbling my way down some rocks onto the glacier. In those first few steps I saw the first crevasse, a frightening wake-up call.

Concentrate. Trust your instincts. Follow the guides. Don't stab yourself with the ice axe!

The moon was several days past full, but the bright light on the snow was reflective enough to show the way. I concentrated hard on each step. I didn't want to slow down the rest of the hikers on my rope team, yet I wanted to be careful not to trip and fall. There was very little talking. Once across a snowy flat, crampons crackling and biting into the icy surface, we started up the rock to Cadaver Gap. It was tricky going, climbing up rock and scree (loose rocks) with crampons in the darkness. I scrambled up and around boulders, falling to my knees many times, trying to keep my balance, feeling the constant tug of the rope that bound me to the climber behind me, the tautness of the line telling me he was already beginning to tire. For some inexplicable reason, the guides put me at the head of the rope. Louie was the fourth member in the rear of the line.

We were soon on the Ingraham ice flat at 11,000 feet and took our first break. During our rest period, I pulled a parka from my backpack because of the cold temperatures. We were working pretty hard during the ascent. The human body can cool off fast, so extra gloves and a pull-down hat were important in order to keep warm. I began to understand why the guides had watched us during training. They were continuing their assessment of which hikers might not make it and should return to Camp Muir while it was an hour or so down the mountain.

I overheard the guide scold one middle-aged man, "I felt the rope getting tight behind me during this last section. If you're going to continue, I don't want to feel that anymore!"

It was harsh and rude, but necessary for the safety of the rest of the team. The guy promised to keep up the pace, but after leaving the rest area, he dropped out and a guide took him back to Muir. Unfortunately, this occurred in our group, too. Dr. Butch was suffering from altitude sickness, a severe headache, and disorientation. He decided to drop out. Margie, a strong hiker at lower elevations, elected not to continue. Her husband, Phil, also decided that the higher elevation and tricky terrain might not be in the cards for him this time. A guide took him down to Camp Muir. Sam, Louie, Benny, and I lumbered on.

As the sun struck the glacier, the snow and ice became almost glossy, and the points of my crampons dug into the surface. The route became steeper. Most of us were at the highest altitude we had ever reached. My breathing was labored, but I had no problem with the effects of the elevation on my body, no headache or nausea. The sun was beginning to peek over the horizon, painting the early-morning sky with a palette of pinks and oranges.

Looking back, I could see that we really were on a path now, a series of severe switchbacks worn smooth by hikers and guides who had been on the mountain all summer. It was warming considerably. The snow was slushy, and the hiking was becoming almost routine.

Just after a short break, at about 14,000 feet and with less than an hour to go before we reached the summit, the Russian guide pulled Sam out of the rope line. I had been watching him, asking how he was feeling. I thought that he was struggling, but we were so close, I knew he could make it to the top. But, unfairly, the guides made the decision that he was in no shape to complete the summit push. He was crushed, and so was his dad. The guides put Sam in his sleeping bag, secured it to the snow, and left him there to be picked up on our way down.

We trudged along and reached what looked like the last stretch to the summit crater. However, with legs and lungs burning, we found ourselves at the top of a small crest, with the true summit still several hundred feet away. At about seven o'clock, we had about 200 yards or so to go.

Then, with no fanfare or blaring trumpets, we made the last few steps to the summit of Mount Rainier.

Louie, Benny, and I embraced and reveled in the accomplishment. Secure against some well-worn rocks, we sat for a moment of pure introspection and relief. I had a few bites of a Power Bar and thought of our friends who hadn't made it. After a photo or two and another long look at the immense height we had attained, we were on our way down.

One of the guides passed along the best survival advice that I used to reach the base of the mountain safely: When you reach the summit of a mountain, you're only halfway there.

In other words, after summiting a peak, you still have to

return safely. Descending is never fun. It's uncomfortable on your knees and back. There is tremendous stress on the joints because for the next 12 hours or more you're headed downhill with very little level ground between you and the bottom of the mountain. Your back also begins to feel the weight of the pack and the equipment.

The excitement of reaching the summit was gone. Benny shouted out to no one in particular, "My knees are killing me," only to have his cry fall on deaf ears. We were all hurting.

The guides were anxious to get down before nightfall. They were constantly calling to us to keep up the pace and be mindful of slack on the line. One fit climber sprained his knee on the way down. He had to be bandaged and hobbled along, slowing down the entire group. Underscoring how fit the guides were, one of them ended up carrying his own pack and the injured hiker's pack all the way to the bottom, a heavy, bulky burden on each shoulder.

I was near exhaustion, though we stopped occasionally for rest. During one break, I hung my helmet over my ice axe. Before I knew it, the helmet had slipped from the pole, scooting down the icy slope, disappearing into the air below. Embarrassed, I looked at the guides, but I was thinking all along, better the helmet than me!

We reached Camp Muir at around two in the afternoon. After a quick drink of water and a bite to eat, we were off for the final push to the base of the mountain. My back and legs screamed with fatigue.

The final few steps were along a paved path. As we rounded the corner, we saw Joe and the support team waiting to greet us with smiles and open arms.

It had been a grand experience. Later that night, an ice-cold bottle of Rainier beer and a delicious rainbow trout was my reward for summiting Mount Rainier. Then, a hot shower, a comfortable bed and a few last thoughts of what I had achieved.

It has been many years since my buddies and I touched the summit of Mount Rainier. For a few months after the climb, I adopted a false sense of braggadocio that didn't serve me well. My comeuppance came shortly. The following summer I failed to summit a relatively easy climb to the top of Snowmass Mountain in Colorado. I lost my nerve on the "mountaineer's route" during an ascent of Mount

McKinley in California and begged my guide to allow me to trek the trail down the mountain instead of taking the more treacherous passage over the side of a sheer wall of rock on one side of the summit. Back in Colorado, I struggled to the summit of Mount Elbert, the tallest mountain in the state at near the height of Mount Rainier.

Despite my later missteps, I have looked back many times with great fondness at the Mount Rainier assault. My memory is strong: I have replayed the steps, the training, the effort, and the advice from those talented guides to the point that sometimes it seems like the ordeal took place only a few weeks ago. It lives with me constantly. I am immediately taken back to the glacier when I hear of a Mount Rainier accident or death. I am sometimes eager, sometimes reluctant to tell someone of my conquest. Summiting Mount Rainier is and will always be a part of who I am and who I've become.

L to Right, Bill, Benny Dickinson, Louie Dickinson and a relative of
Louie's on the summit of Mt. Rainier, Washington

Hiking the snowfield to Camp Muir the day before the summit
climb on Mt. Rainier

Official certification after summiting Mt. Rainier

Reaching the Top: Ascents of Snowmass and Whitney

Ice cold raindrops the size of quarters hopscotched across my forehead, skipping their way around and under the hood of my rain jacket. I was getting soaked and my face hurt. Fortunately, my hiking friends and I were close to the summit of Virginia's Mount Rogers. The mountain is the northernmost habitat of Southern Appalachia's high-altitude spruce-fir forests, found in only five other locations in the United States.

There is something about a pounding rainstorm that drives your thoughts inward. You concentrate on each step, yet your mind wanders—head down, shoulders hunched to give the rain a roadway off your jacket. If a storm lasts long enough, it will cause a man to discuss his most closely guarded secrets with the fellows next to him.

But we had no time for confessionals that afternoon. Arriving at a bald—a flat, smooth piece of ground where we camped for the night—each of us had to scramble to get a tent up and salvage what dry clothes and belongings we could from the ferocious pelting rain. Laconic and unsmiling, we quickly established our shelter.

Years ago, someone told me that people fall into one of two categories: mountain people or ocean people. I've been trying to pigeonhole myself into one of those categories ever since. I love the sea: the breezes, the gulls, and the way the rhythm of the surf can lull even an insomniac into a deep, forgetful sleep. But now I was enthralled by the tallest peak in Colorado. For me and a hardy group of like-minded mortals, it was the mountain, a gargantuan granite formation that had rested, perhaps untested and undiscovered, for millions of years, that called out to us.

Louie, my cousin and an internal medicine specialist from Glasgow, Kentucky, along with Benny, a Barren County Circuit judge, and I had conquered the summit of Mount Rainier in Washington two summers earlier. It had been a grueling endeavor on one of the toughest peaks in the world, but we had done it safely and were proud of the effort. Weekend backpacking trips, like this one to Mount Rogers and numerous other treks on parts of the Appalachian Trail, gave us a chance to discuss other climbing adventures.

After the rain, stripped down and huddled in my sleeping bag, I felt an afternoon snooze coming on. Rain fell steadily. The sound of the trees swaying in the wind lulled me to sleep. I called out that I was going to nap only to find that everyone else was doing the same.

I once read an account of two guys who had bagged the highest peaks in all 50 states. Mount Rogers, elevation 5,719 feet, was their 49th summit. Virginia is a beautiful state and offers much to the outdoorsman, but she greeted us with weather bad enough to send anyone scrambling for a Motel 6. For a fall hike, we had arrived early, only to stare out into the fog at a fallow field with all the enthusiasm that President Clinton must have felt watching his impeachment hearings on television. Forcing ourselves out of a warm vehicle, we ambled through a nearly deserted parking lot into the Mount Rogers National Recreational Area—154,000 protected acres located in the southwest tip of the state named for the allegedly chaste first Queen of England.

We geared up, anxious to get on the way, hopeful that the dense forest would work as an umbrella. The air was brisk, the trailhead dotted with jagged rocks covered with lizard-green moss.

Forty minutes down the trail, we realized that we were lost. Sullen and damp, we returned to the parking lot. We'd taken the opposite direction on the wrong trail. That mistake quickly remedied, we headed up the muddy Rhododendron Trail through a meadow littered with pony poop and granite boulders. Yes, the park service had unleashed feral ponies years ago to roam free in the open meadows of the mountain. In the warm months, they graze the high ridgeline off the Appalachian Trail and are easy to spot, sometimes wandering through tent sites and close to campers eager for photos. In the cooler winter months, the small horses—slightly larger than a Shetland pony—find their way down the mountain knowing that salt blocks and hay from the pony protection patrol wait for them. Isn't it nice to know that in this age of congested interstate highways, iPods and world wars, there is a peaceful, protected place where wild ponies graze unconfined?

Half a mile higher on the mountain, named after Dr. William Barton Rogers, Virginia's first geologist and the founder of Massachusetts Institute of Technology, we turned west on the white-blazed Appalachian Trail to Rhododendron Gap. If you're fortunate enough to arrange a trip to the mountain in early summer, you'll find hundreds of bright rhododendron shrubs painting the mountainside with color. The forests on Mount Rogers are one of the few remaining habitats for the Fraser fir, which is significant because of recent declines due to an infestation from a non-native European insect. Also, some researchers have surmised that air pollution in the form of nitrogen and sulfur compounds originating from nearby power plants has also been a source of stress to the firs.

Hiking in the fog and wind through the forest of Mount Rogers might have been more pleasant with a warmer temperature, but by the time we stumbled to the summit in the late afternoon, we'd grown tired of the chilly downpour. About halfway up the mountain, we passed three wild ponies grazing behind a cluster of stunted trees, took a quick picture, and went on our way. Mountain goats? Ground squirrels? Maybe bear? No, for us, seeing ponies was unusual.

After a nap and a change into a pair of dry socks I had packed, we gathered in the center of the circle of tents that had been hastily erected a couple of hours earlier. Thankfully, the rain had stopped. Mike had split a few sticks of firewood, exposing the dry interior of the wood, and with dry kindling, he had a decent blaze going—enough to dry out our jackets and hiking boots.

Louie fired up his propane stove to boil a pot of water just about the time I had finished my snack, a package of peanut-butter crackers. He glanced up just as the smoke from the fire began to dance among the red spruce trees and with a sheepish grin asked me, "Are you about ready to top out another one?"

"What do you have in mind?"

"Whitney."

I paused and thought, "We'd freeze to death, and I can't take enough time off from work to go to Alaska."

As I peeled back the cover on my freeze-dried fettuccine Alfredo, I replied, "I don't think any of us have the time or inclination to climb Denali. We did well on Rainier, but Whitney is a different story, don't you think?"

Louie looked over at his cousin Benny as if to say, this boy needs a geography lesson, and quickly corrected my mistake. "Mount Whitney—in California—the highest peak in the continental United States—not McKinley in Alaska, Goodman."

Now, I was interested. "Tell me more."

Obviously, I didn't know a lot about Mount Whitney. Over a cup of steaming coffee, with just a splash of Kentucky bourbon, I asked Louie to spell out the details. As expected, he had done his homework.

Louie, who declined to add any coffee to his nightcap, leaned back in his folding camp chair and described the Whitney climb with enthusiasm.

"It's the highest point in the Sierras and all of California. And it rises higher than any piece of land in the United States outside of Alaska. It's a helluva piece of rock."

My thoughts: We're on the highest piece of land in Virginia, and Whitney is over 9,000 feet higher.

Benny chimed in, "I'm in. When do we go?"

Louie continued. "Officially, it's listed as 14,505 feet. From what I've been reading, it's not that tough—there's a trail all the way to the summit, no glaciers, a huge number of people apparently walk it every year. Some run up the damn thing—11 miles up and back in one day—although I say we make it a two-day trip, don't you?"

He threw the question into the face of an increasing chilly breeze, which was stirring the embers in Mike's fire, when he added: "But there's a different route too.

"It's called the Mountaineer's Route. Makes it more of a challenge. Fewer people too. We might want to consider hiring a guide."

Louie didn't lie on purpose—he just had a hard time coming to grips with the exact truth. Ask him how far the Appalachian Trail overnight shelter was, and he'd respond, "Hmmm, about two more miles." That meant the shelter was five miles ahead. Questioned at the beginning of the trail this morning about which way the arrow on the sign was pointing, he had replied, "It's this way. We're okay." Later, we forded a small creek, which appeared shallow from the bank, but was deeper in the middle of the stream than we had anticipated. Louie, looking down as creek water poured into my boot, said, "We probably should have scouted for another crossing."

I perked up when Louie suggested climbing the Mountaineer's Route. It was more challenging, and we'd have a professional guide along. "Just how much of a challenge?" I queried.

He mumbled something about talking about it in the morning.

With that, our dinner party disbanded. As a crisp breeze pushed me toward the tent, a couple of thoughts followed me through the flap and into my sleeping bag.

I flashed back to an unsuccessful climb on Snowmass Mountain just a few months ago.

Snowmass is one of Colorado's fourteeners—more than 50 peaks in the state that stand over 14,000 feet high. Some hearty souls have climbed all of them. Benny, Louie, and I had summited Mount Rainier the summer before and were looking for another challenge. Snowmass is the 34th highest peak in the state, located in the Elk Mountains within the Maroon Bells-Snowmass Wilderness. The mountain is named for a large snowfield that lies on its eastern slopes and shouldn't be confused with the Snowmass ski area and village. It is one of the state's most remote fourteeners. The shortest trail to the base is about 10 miles.

The route to the top seemed simple enough. A rock scramble took you to the snowfield, which led to the ridgeline. The thin knife-edge ridge to the summit jets up about 50 feet from the slopes. The rocks look like spears coming up out of the earth. At the top, careful going is required because of the exposure.

Louie, the trailmeister, had explained to our group of Kentucky flatlanders that it would be the perfect trip. A 10-mile approach the first day, overnight at Snowmass Lake, watch the sun set over the mountain peak, and climb the next day.

One of my best hiking, running, vacationing buddies was Phillip Whiteside. I had glamorized our Mount Rainier trip to the point that Phillip and his daughter Jane Ann had joined our group. I told them I'd stick with them and that we would get to the top together, and, at that point, back in our snug small town, everything seemed good and safe. Although Phillip and I had backpacked up and down several high-altitude passes, we would soon find out that being on a foot trail and hanging out on the side of a mountain were two different levels of exposure.

At dawn the next day, the sun cast long shadows on the east side of the mountain, turning the snowfield a bright pink. The warm rays softened the snow making crampons unnecessary. We carried day packs, water, and a snack. After oatmeal and a Power Bar, we were on our way.

There's no trail to the summit. You simply read the guidebook, head in the right direction, and pick your own route. It's not very scientific, but thousands of other hiker-climbers have done it this way for years. Why not us? So, it was around the lake, across Snowmass Creek, onto a grassy meadow onto the scree. The climbing was invigorating—steep and taxing on the calves—but the brisk, refreshing mountain air made the going easy. There wasn't a cloud in the sky.

We took a rest break near 12,000 feet. A narrow rock outcropping provided just enough security for all of us to relax and sit. The view at that point was spectacular, as if someone had helicoptered us to the top of the Sears Tower. After peanuts and Gatorade, we were off again.

Somehow, we got split up. Mike, his wife, Jess, Louie, and Benny went in one direction around a small stream. Jane Ann, Phillip, and I went the other way around the runoff from the snowfield. Crossing the brook, I suddenly felt unsteady. I slipped and found myself spread-eagle in the middle of the stream. Luckily, the stream was just a trickle, but trying to right myself without sliding down the incline was quite a task.

I heard Phillip yelling, "Hey, where are you?"

Before he could scramble down for the rescue, I jumped to attention, brushed myself off, and joined the other climbers. By that time, the first group was several hundred yards ahead, and left the three of us to pick our way. I overheard a muffled conversation between Jane Ann and her dad about the pitch of the mountainside. We were on a 45 degree grade, not dangerous, but steep enough that you had to bend down with a gloved hand to steady yourself every other step. It was not a spot for the faint of heart.

Jane Ann felt nauseous. At this altitude, she was probably not acclimated. She was scared. That didn't make Phillip feel any better either, and they were both scaring me. We were at 12,500 feet. How was I going to get to the summit of Snowmass and get them down at the same time? The descent route didn't pass this way.

A one-person boulder jutted from beneath the snow about a dozen yards from our position. In the calmest voice I could muster, I said, "Let's get up there, and take a break. We'll decide what to do from there."

Jane Ann had already decided. She was going home. And her daddy was going with her. And her daddy's friend was going with them. It was butt-scootin' time!

After discussing a couple of options—rest and continue up the mountain or abandon plans to summit and head back to camp— Phillip and Jane Ann decided to use the ancient mountain-climbing technique of sliding on one's backside down to safety.

I had a decision to make. Looking up toward the high wall of the ridgeline, the other Kentucky climbers had become wind-up toy soldiers marching toward the summit. If I was going to attempt the peak, I'd be by myself.

I had always been careful, maybe too much so, but proud of my intuition for anticipating trouble. When Louie had leaped at age nine from an overhanging limb into the swirling stormwater at Boy Scout camp, I had hesitated and waited for him to bob to the top before I jumped. In high school, someone else made the first daredevil hurdle off the rock cliff into Barren River Lake. On Rainier, I had made sure I finished first in the self-rescue class. Secretly, I regarded what some called fear as more a kind of ultimate rationality that I possessed.

I went down the mountain, too. We got back to the tents in time to watch the others glissade more than 3000 feet down the mountain slope. We watched our friends plummet from just below the precipice, twisting, turning, laughing hysterically as they zoomed down the hump of snow. I watched silently, full of regret.

We made plans throughout the long Kentucky winter to summit Mount Whitney the following August. We picked up Sam as an additional member of the group. Sam, Benny's son, younger and stronger than any of us, had failed to reach the top of Mount Rainier on the trip we'd taken to the West Coast two years before, and he had struggled since then with that demon of regret. We flew to Las Vegas, grabbed a rental car, and drove across Death Valley. What an aberrant, desolate habitat, 110 degrees in the daytime and freezing at night. Passing Badwater, the lowest elevation in the United States, we made a mental note to check the gas tank before our return trip. At Lone Pine, California, with the foreboding granite walls of Mount Whitney staring down at us, we found a cheap motel. Later, I took my old friends—fear and trepidation—to bed with me.

Early the next morning, we drove the winding road to the Whitney Portal. In 1864, the peak was named after Josiah Whitney, a California state geologist. The most popular route to the summit goes up the Whitney Trail, a 22-mile round trip with an elevation gain of over 6100 feet. Of course, that's the easy way. We would take the Mountaineer's Route, a gully scramble and technical climb on the north side of the east face first climbed by famed hiker and outdoorsman John Muir. The steep eastern side of the mountain offered a variety of climbing challenges.

During the summer, the approach takes hikers over trails, through towering pine forests, over boulders, around dramatic drop-offs with granite slabs as big as train cars, high alpine meadows, and lakes as cold as ice water.

At the Whitney Portal parking lot, we met one of the kindest, most professional mountain guides in the business. Kurt Wedberg, a California beach-boy type with a lot of hair, dressed the part of a mountain climber with cool climbing shoes and a North Face jacket pulled up tight around his neck. He was the founder of Sierra Mountaineering International based in Bishop, California. He'd been guiding and instructing in the Sierras, Joshua Tree, and other countries worldwide since 1986. He had gotten a lot of training as a guide on Mount Rainier and had summited peaks in Alaska, Argentina and Ecuador, and had successfully climbed in the Himalayas. He had reached the top of Mount Everest twice.

After introductions, Kurt abruptly said, "Let's see what you have in your packs." We hauled our 50-pounders out of the van. "Dump them out," said Kurt.

Whoa! I had spent hours in the motel room packing just the right amount of food, raingear, and my air mattress into tiny little cubbyholes and hiding places. Kurt pointed out that human beings make miserable pack mules and, yet, every year thousands of hikers set out for the mountains with overstuffed packs. The weight of a backpack can cause stooping, fatigue, and loss of balance, and while we might have conquered Mount Rainier once, Kurt quickly discovered we were poor packers.

He reached into my bag and began discarding socks, T-shirts, and hats left and right. He wanted to be sure the backpack rested comfortably just above our hip bones, which Benny had a hard time finding. After that he equally distributed the food and gear he had brought along: ropes, carabiners (a D-shaped ring with a spring catch on one side used for fastening ropes), pitons (metal spikes you hammered in the rock wall so a rope could be passed through an eyelet), and pasta, sauce, oatmeal, dried chicken, raisins, nuts, and a mix for chocolate cake we would enjoy the night of our summit.

I pumped Kurt for his life story as we huffed those first few hundred feet up the path.

"I've been climbing since I was a kid. Instead of baseball or golf, my dad took me to the mountains. I went to California State Northridge and got a political science degree, but worked my way through school teaching rock climbing, backpacking. The summer I graduated I got a job with the RMI, the guide service on Mount Rainier."

Kurt had been guiding professionally for 10 years. If he worked 200-plus days a year, he could make a decent living. I liked him and thought he had a reassuringly cautious outlook. I felt more comfortable and confident being in his shadow for this trip.

I did ask one more question. "What is the scariest thing that has happened to you as a guide?"

Kurt didn't hesitate. "I've had one near-death experience in all my years of guiding. I was leading a rope team of three, including myself, on a Mount Rainier climb. The gal behind me got blown off her feet in a gust of wind. I self-arrested and stopped her, but in the process we had pulled the last guy, a hefty fella, off-balance. He slid down and gained enough momentum so that when the rope went tight—the force pulled me off my stance. I tried to self-arrest and bring us to a stop, but I ran out of time, and all three of us fell into a crevasse. The two of them fell about 40 feet and hit a false bottom. I hit a different spot about 60 feet down. Knocked me out. When I came to, I climbed up to them and made sure they were okay and then climbed out. I had some help with their rescue from there."

"Was everybody okay?"

"Yep, lucky, couple of bruises, and the girl broke a bone in her wrist. It shouldn't have happened, but I did the best I could."

Kurt had the people skills and solid mountaineering experience to be a great guide. He was already proving it.

By mid-morning, we were making good time. I breathed in deeply, reveling in hiking, methodically putting one foot in front of the other, shifting the pack occasionally to correct a muscle cramp or pain, lost in the blanket of green and gray that surrounded us as we climbed.

On the Whitney Trail, Kurt made a sharp right turn into the brush, with us following. I thought we were trail hiking, but we were in the bush with no worn footpath. We crossed a stream at the bottom of the valley and wound our way above the willow trees. As the valley narrowed and steepened, we carved our way through coarse brush that grabbed at our packs and pants.

Kurt yelled out above the low roar of water tumbling over boulders: "We're headed for the Ebersbacher Ledges, which will get us out of these willows," and he pointed with his trekking pole at an ominous-looking rock wall ahead.

To navigate the ledges, you maneuver over a sliver of a loose rock walkway for 50 feet or so until the path empties into thin air. At that point you're staring down at the stream 200 feet below. I was one of the team carrying 50 feet of mountain climbing rope, and I wondered why Kurt had not roped us at this point. From up above, he shouted, "Grab the roots of that pine, swing your leg about two feet to the right—yeah, yeah, that foothold. Now, pull yourself up until you can get your left foot in that crack. See it?"

We clambered over boulders, careful not to lose our balance or turn an ankle. Before long, we entered a spare valley that led to Iceberg Lake at 12,600 feet. Slinging my backpack, I glanced east past the water, up the snowfield through the stony notch, up, up, my neck craning to see what appeared to be a sheer rock wall that Kurt said was our summit destination.

After we put up tents and added a warm layer of clothing, jackets, and wool hats, Kurt pointed toward the mountain, explaining the route we would follow the next morning. Our early arrival at camp ensured we had plenty of time to think about Whitney's imposing east face.

As I had admitted earlier, I am a bit cautious, even a worrier. The outcome of any venture in the mountains is uncertain. Weather often has the final say on a climb's success, but many other things can go wrong as well. I always worry I've forgotten some valuable piece of equipment or will get a last-minute cold or stomach upset. At high elevation, the altitude is a worry, as the slightest headache can develop into something more serious. Camping at Iceberg Lake set us up for the next day's route, but it also placed a lot of strain on our bodies, which were not acclimated.

Make it through the night in good shape, and I reckon I'll be solid for the climb, I thought. But after our camp dinner, I couldn't help but be transfixed by that immense wall of rock. As the sky darkened and the night settled in, I drifted off to sleep wondering if I'd pushed myself a little too far this time.

Kurt's alarm rattled at 4:30. He fired up his stove to brew coffee and oatmeal.

The morning air was quiet, cold, clear, and windless. Moonlight shone on the rocky talus and dark spires above. We packed quietly.

The blue-white beam from my headlamp bobbed off the stony floor as we left Iceberg Lake. There hadn't been much conversation. Kurt tried to chat with us, but we were quiet, consumed by our own thoughts, trying not to think too much about the day ahead.

On summit day, you're supposed to be fired up, excited to the point that courage and skill tap down the knot in your stomach. Am I the only one who feels this?

We crossed the talus and headed toward the snowfield. In 30 minutes, we paused to strap on crampons that helped us bite and chew our way up the snow. Kurt roped us up—harness belted, rope looped, carabineer locked. Behind us, the eastern sky began its daily magic show. Lone Pine Peak's silhouette rose above the Owen

Valley. As we began to clang across the rocks to the crusty snow, the moon slipped behind Whitney's towering mass, and the rock was just starting to show a hint of pink.

I began to relax. We had been on a rope team before and soon found a steady rhythm. Kurt was in the lead, then me, Sam, Benny, and Louie. Before long, we were at the notch between the two towers, a narrow cut between the colossal slabs of granite that rose several hundred feet above us. Kurt timed our arrival perfectly. Resting in the arms of the notch, we huddled together and gazed at Iceberg Lake below— a tiny puddle with three green tents on its icy shore. The opposite side of the cut offered only a sheer drop of a thousand vertical feet to the distant moraines below. The jagged talus down there appeared as fine grains of sand on a grayish beach.

"We're going up there," Kurt gestured. "Give me a few minutes to climb ahead, check out the route, look for the fixed pitons—be sure no one has rearranged the furniture." He searched the face of the 400-foot rock wall for his first foothold. From this vantage point, we couldn't see the summit; the wall seemed to slant at an odd angle toward the east, toward us, bending over slightly at the crown.

In a few minutes, he had climbed back down to us. Crampons off, we awaited further instruction. Kurt checked our climbing harnesses, double-checked knots, cinched belts tighter, and we were on our way. He led the first traverse up and across the wall, looking for foot and hand-holds, reaching a point where he could tie off the rope on a secure boulder.

Somehow I remembered the advice about not looking down, and I kept my eyes fixed on the next step ahead. I listened intently to Kurt's suggestions on where to place my fingers to grasp a knot of rock that could provide the ballast I needed to lift my body to the next step. Only once or twice did I glance downward, over my shoulder, to my buddies below me. As rope team members, we talked to each other, suggesting the same rock steps that Kurt suggested.

Just past midmorning, a glimpse toward the top told me the wall was beginning to slant away. A great expanse of blue exploded above.

"How's it looking, Kurt?" I shouted.

"Not too much more to go. Watch that rock—it wiggles a little."

Clutching for handholds, I made my way to a tapered ledge and waited for the others to catch up. From there, we stepped onto a series of granite ledges. As much as I had enjoyed the constant buzz of exposure, I was ready to stand on solid ground.

I heard muffled conversation and realized it was coming from the top. In minutes, we scrambled up the final few boulders. Kurt beckoned, encouraged me, and I straightened up and kissed the summit of Mount Whitney.

We shared a group hug and a photo at the peak. The summit surface is about two or three football fields in length and width, piled with rock of every imaginable size and description. It has a stone hut, built by the park service decades ago to give shelter during the violent storms that occur frequently. Other hikers had come up the Whitney Trail or another route, but no one had crisscrossed the wall of the Mountaineer's Route. We had soloed it that morning.

As storm clouds began to form, we ate some raisins and drank water before the descent. Shards of hail began to pour down, and Kurt hurried us over the edge of the Whitney rooftop, down the wall to our camp at Iceberg Lake. Roped once more, I carefully picked my way down the mountain, through the notch, sinking into the mushy snowfield, to the much-anticipated chocolate cake.

A group of fathers and sons on the summit of Mt. Whitney, California

On the summit of Uncompahgre Peak, the sixth highest summit in Colorado

L to R: Phillip Whiteside, Bill, Phil Patton at Buckskin Pass, a 12,462 ft. trail towering above the Maroon Bells-Snowmass Mountains near Aspen, Col.

Bill and Phillip Whiteside in the Colorado mountains

L to R: On the mountaineers route to the summit of Mt. Whitney in California, Benny Dickinson, Sam Dickinson, Louie Dickinson, Bill

Hiking out of a winter snowfall in the Great Smoky Mountains near Newfound Gap, Tn.

Acknowledgments

I would like to express my gratitude to the many people who saw me through this book; to all of those who provided support, read, critiqued, edited, offered comments, allowed me to quote their remarks and tell these stories.

I was blessed with a wonderful mother and father and I honor them in this very small way by telling you a little about them. Glasgow, in Barren County, Kentucky, is a main character too; it gave me roots and a place I'll always call home.

I want to recognize the many friends and relatives—cousins, aunts, the Trigg family, and George and Naomi Hall—who are integral participants in the essays.

How could I've written any of the words about backpacking and climbing without the close relationships and memories one collects on the trail with his friends?

A special thanks to Harriet and Dero Downing and their many contributions in writing about Joe Downing's life. It was immensely helpful to have access to the archive material and interviews at Western Kentucky University in Bowling Green, Kentucky.

To the mentors, classmates and faculty at Spalding University's MFA program in Louisville, I tip my hat—you brought me here.

A hug and appreciation to my sister Trigg Vance, who gave me a tough edit, correcting some colloquial spelling and facts. I could not have done it without you, Sis.

Last and not least: my wife Debbie: editor, computer guru, and confidant, who pushed, supported and loved me every step of the way.

About the Author

Bill Goodman is the host and managing editor of *Kentucky Tonight* on Kentucky Educational Television. Additionally, he serves as host for *Education Matters* and the conversation show *One to One with Bill Goodman*. He also writes the KET blog "Bill's Eye."

A native of Glasgow, Kentucky, Goodman earned his MFA in Creative Nonfiction from Spalding University in November 2012. In April 2013, he was inducted into the Kentucky Journalism Hall of Fame.

His essays have been published in *The Louisville Review*, *New Madrid: Journal of Contemporary Literature* and *Life's Vivid Creations*, a publication of the Marysville Community and Technical College.

Bill and his wife Debbie reside in Lexington, Ky.

Made in the USA
Lexington, KY
12 January 2017